GUIDE
WINNING
THE POOLS

ROSTERS LTD

GUIDE TO WINNING THE POOLS

Dennis Jones

ROSTERS LTD

Published by Rosters Ltd
60 Welbeck St
London, W1

First edition 1989

ISBN 0 948032 49 9

Filmset by Gwynne Printers, Hurstpierpoint, West Sussex
Printed and bound in Great Britain by Cox & Wyman Ltd, Reading

Foreword

The first time I met the author of this book, he was doing what I've since learnt he does best. He was studying the redeeming features of the pool, his concentration at its keenest checking out the one with the best perm, most expressive figure and superior line – then 'splash', and the sun-kissed tropical beauty hit the deep end! That was Palma, Majorca, 1980. The pool – that of the swimming kind – but it wasn't long before the conversation, courtesy of the odd 'cerveza' or two, turned to that of the jackpot variety.

Dennis, a former TV sports reporter, with a background of wartime football with Queens Park Rangers and a post-war spell with Headington United (now Oxford) talked a good game! He convinced me that 'winning the pools' was a very viable possibility – he'd even gone into print to prove it. 'The Pools Punter's Guide to a Fortune' was the title of his book and its aim quite simple – to help all those cross-sections of society who try their luck at finding those ever-elusive eight score-draws.

Why does Dennis give all his secrets away? Philanthropy gone mad? No! But he feels that his systems can earn the average punter a more regular return from filling in the coupon. On the very day the book first appeared in the shops, Dennis produced a first dividend cheque. Since then winning vouchers have consistently dropped through his letter-box – including two substantial four-figure wins. Letters of approval have also poured in from readers lucky with their coupons since reading Dennis's chapter and verse.

He doesn't promise the impossible – but, says an Edinburgh University professor of mathematics, 'He decreases peoples chances of not winning'. He even gave me a permutation – that couldn't fail! It has – consistently! – basically because I've never got myself into the habit of filling in the blessed coupon. Nevertheless, having read the draft of this newer, bigger, better and more comprehensive edition of his book my appetite has been whetted . . . and now the pen is poised over the pools coupon every Thursday.

Brian Barwick
(Editor, BBC TV 'Match of the Day')

P.S. By the way, if you've always wanted to meet the bloke who spends his last 25 pence in change on a raffle ticket and three months later wins first prize . . . a brand new car, I've met him . . . that's Dennis, lucky so and so.

P.P.S. Is that his next book?

Contents

Introduction 8

Chapter One: Changing the coupon 14

Chapter Two: Getting started 16

Chapter Three: Increasing your chance of success 19

Chapter Four: The winning formula 21

Chapter Five: The positive approach 24

Chapter Six: Dennis' pet perm 102

Chapter Seven: Checking your pools 108

Chapter Eight: Beating 'Sod's Law' 112

Chapter Nine: Making the most of your 'Lucky Numbers' 115

Chapter Ten: The luck of the draw 117

Introduction

I first took a serious interest in the football pools some years ago when I lived in Oxford. At that time my working week consisted of travelling to schools in Oxfordshire, Berkshire and Buckinghamshire teaching football under the Football Association's Coaching Scheme, in addition to which I had a private contract coaching the youngsters at the Christ Church Cathedral school. However, as the coaching sessions were only of about one hour duration, I had plenty of time on my hands, whilst at the same time money was at a premium. I decided that the only way I could augment my meagre income was to win the pools. Admittedly this was a mere 'pipe-dream' and one which I undoubtedly shared with millions of other people.

I had always taken an interest in gambling having been part-owner of a race-horse, which despite being a good jumper, could never run quite fast enough between the 'sticks'. I also had a greyhound called 'Magic Boy', with which I enjoyed a good measure of success. But winning the pools presented me with a real challenge. The more I thought about it, the more I felt there must be some way to win other than merely relying 100% on 'Dame Fortune' smiling kindly. So I decided to make a serious study of the football results for the next few weeks, in particular taking special notice of the pattern in which the draws fell. And it was through doing this that the embryo of my system was born.

However, I needed to make absolutely certain that

the particular pattern which I had discovered remained constant, so I checked back over five years results, and was more than happy with the outcome. But having made what to my mind, was an exciting discovery, the next problem was how to apply it to the pools coupon. Following hours of study and juggling with figures, I eventually hit on a system which has stood the test of time to my complete satisfaction.

My first-ever win on the Treble Chance was equivalent today to a modest £500, but this was quickly followed a few weeks later by a more respectable cheque equivalent to £4,690, with a few minor dividends sandwiched in between. It was at about this time that I decided to move down to Cornwall, being influenced by someone at the Football Association's H.Q., who informed me that there was plenty of work available in the area under their 'coaching scheme'. So with the money I'd won, I scraped together enough to buy a cottage and borrowed £2,500 from my bank for renovations. Today the cottage is worth around £50,000.

The exercise turned out to be a case of 'The best-laid plans of mice and men oft go awry', because on arriving in the West Country, I learned from the local F.A. secretary that schools in Cornwall didn't require qualified F.A. Coaches, as they all had their own football teachers. I thought to myself that it was no wonder Cornwall was such a 'hot-bed' of soccer. It could also be the answer as to why such a large county as Cornwall has never, and to my mind will never, muster a side capable of providing its long suffering football fans with league football. When Penzance F.C. offered me a part-time coaching job I accepted with alacrity. In addition to this post I was appointed Scout for Devon and Cornwall by Swindon Town F.C.

Despite the slim coaching pickings, I was confident that the Treble Chance would augment a very meagre income and was soon rewarded for my optimism. I went over to Newquay one Saturday afternoon to watch a player on behalf of Swindon Town, and after the game bought an evening paper to check on the football results. Despite the glorious weather we were enjoying in the west country, I was dismayed on reading the results to see that a number of matches had been postponed due to the water-logged state of the grounds. I was very disappointed as with so many postponements, I thought I had no chance of winning. However, a closer inspection of the results revealed only six draws – and I knew I had them all. I wasn't 100% certain that they all fell in my three-block full perm – and I'd left my copy coupon at home. My original intention had been to visit friends in Newquay that evening, instead of which I changed my plans and broke all speed records in getting back to my home near Penzance.

On arrival I needed only a quick glance at my copy coupon to know I'd won – with maximum points. The following day I saw from the Sunday paper that telegram claims were required for maximum points, so I hot-footed it to the nearest kiosk and sent mine off.

On Thursday following, the postman brought me a cheque equivalent to £18,050 with which I was more than happy. However, my bank manager at

Henley-on-Thames had been sending me demands for money to pay off my overdraft, so I decided to deliver the cheque personally. The outcome of my visit to the bank manager (with whom I was on reasonably friendly terms), was that he asked if he could come into partnership with me on my system. I answered with an emphatic, but polite, 'NO!'.

In Cornwall, during the summer months, I took holiday-makers on fishing trips in a boat I owned. In the September following my £18,050 win I was down on the boat in Penzance harbour one Sunday hopefully planning to induce some of the few remaining holiday makers wandering around the harbour to come on a fishing trip – but without any success – when one of my rivals, named Charlie Hitchins, came up to me bemoaning the lack of business. I said to him – 'I don't give a damn' – or words to that effect, – 'because I've won the pools.'

Charlie wouldn't believe me. He even asked if he could see the cheque when it arrived. On the following Thursday honour was satisfied when I produced a cheque equivalent to £6,780, with which I promptly bought a nice second-hand 'Jag'. The following Sunday, with just a touch of sarcasm in his voice, Charlie said 'I suppose you're going to tell me you've won again', and I was able to reply in the affirmative.

This time though he really didn't believe me until I produced a cheque for £2,450 the following Thursday. When on the next Thursday I showed him yet another cheque, this time for £780, he really thought I must have been printing the cheques myself. Unfortunately, I've never been able to repeat this 'hat-trick' of wins, but I am forever optimistic.

With things being 'a bit thin on the ground' the following winter I took a job in Harrod's sports department for a few weeks before Christmas. Apart from enjoying the 'after hours' social life during this period, which consisted mainly of parties organised by the 'Debs' who worked in the adjacent toy department in order to earn a bit of extra Christmas money, I also enjoyed a modicum of success on the Treble Chance.

During my stay with Harrods, I earned no prizes for being at work on time in the morning. One day I arrived even later than usual feeling very much like 'the morning after the night before', which evidently showed. As I slumped into the chair at my desk it was to the accompaniment of caustic remarks from the regular assistants, and assistant buyer. In order to keep the peace I offered to buy everyone a drink after work, at one of the two very excellent pubs situated very conveniently opposite Harrods main entrance, alas no longer there. Someone then piped up 'Oh, he must have won the pools', which was a very sensible remark, because with all due deference to the firm, my pay at that time did not really extend to such extravagant gestures. Anyway, I was able to confirm in a not-too-loud voice, that I had in fact won the pools, albeit not very much, because that week there were 16 draws.

Nevertheless, on the following Thursday I was able to ask the buyer if he could cash me a cheque equivalent to £1,200 today in order to buy drinks all round after closing time. Then about a fortnight later, I arrived extremely late, even by my standards, on the Thursday morning. One of the staff suggested I'd been on the 'razzle' the night before to celebrate winning the pools again. I didn't comment, but just said to the buyer (who incidentally didn't appear to mind about the waywardness of his temporary assistant), in a somewhat facetious tone 'Do you think you could cash me a small cheque as I have a date tonight but haven't any cash?'. He said he could manage it, but asked how much I wanted. I presented him with a cheque signed by Zetters Pools for the equivalent of £4,860! Needless to say, there was a snake-like procession across to the pub in Brompton Road immediately after work – led, of course, by yours truly.

Well, that is how I started my pools winning career. Apart from the financial rewards, one of the sweet pleasures of winning the Treble Chance is that of having pitted my brain and wits against odds which, prior to my 'study in depth' of the subject, I thought were so formidable as to be unbeatable.

Dennis Jones

CHAPTER ONE: 'CHANGING THE COUPON'

For the past two decades the format of the pools coupon has comprised 55 matches, but as from the end of the 1985-6 season the number of coupon matches has been increased to 58. To the unsuspecting investor this may appear to be a curious yet insignificant change. Curious because in order to make up even 55 matches the pools coupon compilers have resorted to including non-league games played by clubs few pools punters are likely to know. For instance, on 25th January (1986) the coupon comprised only 20 league games, the remaining 35 made up with such 'high profile (sic)' teams as R.S. Southampton – a Royal Navy Ship's side perhaps, but certainly no relation of 1st Division Southampton, and Mile Oak – a team perhaps made up of New Forest verderers!

In fact, so parochial were the teams listed on the coupon that the BBC Grandstand declined to include them in their Saturday afternoon 'results' slot. Even an ordnance survey motoring atlas could not reveal the wherabouts of some of these teams – which is also the case for the 31 non-league matches making up the larger part of coupon dated 18th February 1989. For example, apart from people living in the vicinity of Birmingham few pools' investors are likely to know the location of Moor

Green.

The inclusion of such 'village' sides makes a complete mockery of the football coupon which the 16 million pools'-investing public justifiably expect to comprise English, Scottish and Welsh league clubs. Indeed, these coupons featuring non-league clubs must ruin the enjoyment of many punters who hitherto derived much pleasure from weighing up the pros and cons of sides with household names before arriving at their Treble Chance selections.

The only remedy I can suggest is for punters to vote with their pens and boycott those dominated by non-league clubs. Why, I wonder, despite their inability to produce a coupon comprising 55 league matches, have the P.P.A. increased the coupon number to 58? Could it be that the forecast I made on many radio stations throughout the U.K. when the first edition of this book was published in 1980 has made its mark? I argued that if every punter followed the advice in my book the number of winners would increase a hundredfold – thereby causing a big slump in the dividends. Insignificant though the increase of three matches may appear, it has in effect made the the winning of the Treble Chance almost 60% more difficult (57.4% to be exact). This will inevitably result in less winners and bigger dividends!

Nevertheless every cloud has a silver lining. Having taken into account this radical change of format in the following chapters I am confident that my readers will ultimately benefit by way of winning larger dividends. So don't delay, read on . . .

CHAPTER TWO: GETTING STARTED

There can be few more exhilarating experiences for a Treble Chance 'pools investor' than that of telephoning a claim for maximum points. But despite filling in a coupon week-in and week-out throughout the year, the vast majority go a lifetime without ever enjoying this pleasure.

However, after both reading and digesting the contents of this book, I feel sure that not only will many readers get far more enjoyment from checking their pools on a Saturday evening, and at the same time find it a far more worthwhile 'chore', but also that a goodly proportion will find themselves in the happy position of being able to send off that winning claim once in a while.

Winning the Treble Chance is the pipe-dream of about 16 million investors every week. Many use 'hit and miss' systems such as lucky numbers, birthday dates, relative's ages etc., while the vast majority pit their wits against the 'form book'. But whatever method is employed in their search for 8 score-draws, most investors use the resultant selections against one of the many 'plans' or 'perms' which are so much in evidence both in the national press, and on the coupons themselves, every week.

However, the cold hard facts are that on the football pools, as in every other walk of life, 'you gets what you pays for'. Sadly, the chances of eight score-draws falling in a line on any of these 'conditional' plans and perms are minimal. By 'conditional' I mean those plans and perms which guarantee 6 or 7 score-draws falling in line should you include 8 or 9 amongst your selections. For instance, one particular so-called 'Super Plan' involves using 18 selections in 1,264 lines, with a guarantee that with 8 correct, 7 score-draws will fall in line. Yet anyone using this particular plan can have little cause to get too excited should they find 8 score-draws amongst their selections, because against the 1,264 lines of which this plan consists, there are 43,758 different ways in which your 8 score-draws **could** line up.

To give you some idea of the comparative futility of using 'conditional' plans and perms, there is one particular plan popularised by a Sunday Newspaper which allows for 36 selections in 1,935 lines. There are in fact 30,260,340 (thirty million, two hundred and sixty thousand three hundred and forty) different ways in which 8 draws can fall in 36 selections, so the chances of 8 draws falling together within a paltry 1,935 lines are considerably less than those of a snowball in hell.

In fact, I suggest many readers will be both amazed and enlightened after studying the 'Full Cover' permutation table on page 23. The short-comings of 'conditional-type' perms and plans becomes clear when you compare the number of lines taken up by any particular perm or plan, with the actual number of lines required to cover the same number of selections with a full orthodox perm.

After reading this book however, I am hopeful that readers will tackle the Treble Chance with new-found optimism and well-founded confidence.

CHAPTER THREE: INCREASING YOUR CHANCE OF SUCCESS

Being a firm believer in the adage 'Little fish are sweet' (or if you prefer – 'A little bit of bread is better than none'), I recommend using the pools firms which afford the greatest chance of success.

On the 8/9th penny per line pool you get 112 lines for each £1 staked, on the 2/9th penny a line, 450 to the £1, and for the 1/15th penny a line, 1,500 lines to the £1, so obviously the lowest stake pool provides infinitely the greater chance of winning. Furthermore, although the dividends are considerably smaller on the lower stake pools, the three major firms each pay around the same pro-rata stake money, i.e. Littlewoods 'Jackpot' is in excess of a million pounds, Vernons about half a million, whilst Zetters 'Tops' hovers around the £80,000 mark.

However, the firm with whom you wish to invest is entirely a matter of personal choice. It must be said in favour of Vernons and Littlewoods that against the 4 dividends paid by Zetters, they pay 5 and 6 respectively. Nevertheless, apart from personal preference, your final choice as to which pools firm you invest with will probably be determined by the number of lines you wish to use allied to the size of your pocket.

Although the majority of pools' investors are far from naive, I feel that very few of the millions using anything other than 'Full Cover' perms each week had, prior to studying the table on page 23, the slightest idea as to how remote are the chances of their favourite plan or perm lining up 8 score-draws to produce 24 points.

A large part of the enjoyment and fascination of 'doing the pools' stems from the excitement of checking your entry. What can be more disappointing than to discover on having trapped 8 or even 9 score-draws – a difficult enough task in itself – that the first dividend has eluded you because they don't line up against your 'conditional' plan or perm.

If you follow the advice I give, you will be able to enjoy the thrill of checking your pools and not have to endure the disappointment of finding that your 8 score-draws don't fall in a line.

CHAPTER FOUR: THE WINNING FORMULA

There is only one certain method of ensuring 8 score-draws falling in line, and this is by using a full cover perm. However, even if you could afford the outlay, I do not recommend this method on 14 selections or more because I do not consider 'full perms' to be good value for money. With a full perm so many lines are virtually wasted. For instance, take an arbitrary figure of 16 selections. What are the chances of your very first 8 selections being all correct, or the very last 8, or the first and last 4, or all the odd numbers, or the even numbers? In point of fact, the odds against 8 score-draws falling in a completely symmetrical pattern are less than remote.

Notwithstanding my opinion, some investors may still opt for using a full orthodox perm. So for their benefit the following table gives the number of lines involved, together with the cost on each of the major pools firms, (these have been rounded up to the nearest penny) for 12 selections up to 16.

Beyond 16 selections the cost of a full perm escalates dramatically and is far beyond the reach of most investors. However, for those readers interested, it can be worked out from the 'full perm' table on page 23.

	No. lines	Littlewoods	Vernons	Zetters
Any 8 from 12	495	£4.40	£1.10	33p
Any 8 from 13	1,287	£11.44	£2.86	86p
Any 8 from 14	3,003	£26.70	£6.68	£2.00
Any 8 from 15	6,435	£57.20	£14.30	£4.29
Any 8 from 16	12,870	£114.40	£28.60	£8.58

Most readers selecting in excess of 16 matches, use one of the numerous plans or perms the virtues of which are extolled every week in the 'Pools Pages' of the national and provincial press and also on the pools coupons themselves. Granted to the layman, they look attractive, with such 'carrot-dangling' as one particular perm involving 18 selections, which guarantees if you only have half correct you will be certain of 7 score-draws falling in line. This is just one example of many, but is to my way of thinking, a very negative approach. Your target should be 8 score-draws and NOT the consolation prizes.

These types of perm are undoubtedly cleverly worked out, but the guarantees offered are akin to a racing tipster, who whilst admitting to having little idea of the winner, offers the consolation of possibly being able to name the 2nd or 3rd horse. What the majority of investors really want, be it in racing or football pools is advice on finding THE WINNER. Regardless of the 'carrots' offered with your favourite plan or perm, the fact remains that there is no conceivable way of deriving a perm which will guarantee 8 draws in-a-line should you nominate 8 amongst your selections except in the case of a full orthodox perm.

The following table gives the number of lines required for full cover from 9 to 32 matches – with 36 included as a matter of hypothetical interest. It also illustrates the enormity of the escalation once the 30's are reached.

Full Permutation Table

Number of Selections	*Lines Required*
8 DRAWS FROM 9	9
" " " 10	45
" " " 11	165
" " " 12	495
" " " 13	1,287
" " " 14	3,003
" " " 15	6,435
" " " 16	12,870
" " " 17	24,310
" " " 18	43,758
" " " 19	75,582
" " " 20	125,970
" " " 21	203,490
" " " 22	319,770
" " " 23	490,314
" " " 24	735,471
" " " 25	1,081,575
" " " 26	1,562,275
" " " 27	2,220,075
" " " 28	3,108,105
" " " 29	4,292,145
" " " 30	5,852,925
" " " 31	7,888,725
" " " 32	10,518,300
" " " 36	30,260,340

CHAPTER FIVE: THE POSITIVE APPROACH

In order to make a determined all-out assault on the Treble Chance, a really positive approach must be made. As readers will already have gathered, this does not include the use of 'conditional' perms or plans (ie, those which guarantee 6 or 7 draws falling in line provided you include 8 or 9 among your selections.)

However, first things first. This chapter deals with the all-important factor of making your selections, and then gets down to the crux of the whole subject – which is to settle on a method of applying the selections to a coupon in such a way that should you 'trap' 8 score-draws, you will not have to endure the agonies and frustration of wondering whether they will line up with your perm.

If all the so-called 'form' draws came up trumps every Saturday, dividends wouldn't be worth a light. So make up your mind to lay as little emphasis as possible on 'form' by mixing likely-looking draws with what appear to be 'home bankers' – whilst at the same time never neglecting 'away bankers'.

This requires a certain amount of will-power to begin with, but the wisdom of this advice will become very apparent after a week or two. You have only to compare the 16 or so Treble Chance 'specials' selected by the pundits in the national newspaper sports pages on a Tuesday or Wednesday, with the results on the ensuing week-end to confirm the fact that if they have managed to forecast 25-30% of the score-draws, then they have done exceptionally well.

A fact which is well worth bearing in mind is that EVERY match on the coupon is a potential score-draw. Having (I hope) convinced readers that it is futile starting at the top of the coupon and putting an X against all the 'form draws', the remainder of this chapter is devoted to explaining a proven method of finding the score-draws, together with explaining a sensible, positive and constructive approach which should put you on the road to at least a modicum of success as a 'pools' investor'.

Eighty per cent of the score-draws week after week and year after year fall in three of the five divisions (taking the Scottish matches as one division). Records over the last 15 years prove this to be a consistent average – a factor which if applied to your Treble Chance entry, is a very solid stepping-stone to success.

Discovery of this factor is tantamount to a professional gambler getting 'inside information' thus enabling him to 'pinch the odds'. To enlarge on this, look at it logically in the following way. Suppose there are 10 score-draws included in the full list of 58 matches – then records prove that on average 8 of these will fall within 3 of the leagues (which comprise 33 or 34 matches). So, mathematically, it is obviously a far easier proposition to pick 8 score-draws from 33 or 34 matches than it is to select 8 out of the full list of 58. In fact with 10 score-draws on the coupon the ratio of 8 draws in three divisions is about 1 in 4, as against the complete coupon ratio of 1 in 5½. Making use of this factor is in my opinion a vital ingredient, but there is one obvious snag in confining your selections to three leagues – namely that of knowing which of the three divisions to select. There are in fact 10 different combinations of three leagues out of five, and these are as follows:

1st Division	2nd Division	3rd Division
1st Division	2nd Division	4th Division
1st Division	2nd Division	Scottish
1st Division	3rd Division	4th Division
1st Division	3rd Division	Scottish
1st Division	4th Division	Scottish
2nd Division	3rd Division	4th Division
2nd Division	3rd Division	Scottish
2nd Division	4th Division	Scottish
3rd Division	4th Division	Scottish

Incidentally, when non-league clubs are included on the coupon, I suggest combining these with division 3 and/or 4. It is obviously impossible to use all the combinations – unless you have limitless funds available – but providing commonsense, perseverance and above all patience is applied, then finding the correct three divisions fairly frequently throughout the season is not an insurmountable problem.

To begin with, very rarely do all the score-draws fall in one half of the coupon, so to all intents and purposes, combinations of the 1st, 2nd and 3rd divisions can be eliminated, likewise the 3rd, 4th and Scottish. Rarely a week goes by without either the 1st or 2nd divisions containing three or more score-draws, but not very often do they both include a surfeit of 3-pointers. So for starters I suggest using just one of the first two divisions. The same principle applies to the 3rd and 4th divisions – one or the other usually comes up with a few score-draws, so it is logical to include one or the other.

If you decide on using the 3rd division (with either the 1st or 2nd), then your final choice lies between the 4th and Scottish. Dividends are nearly always higher when 'North of the Border' matches include a couple or so of score-draws, but on the other hand the 4th division produces a slightly higher average of 3-pointers – so take your pick.

If however you choose one of the first two divisions with division 4, then you are left with 'Hobsons Choice' for your third league. Contrary to a popular myth amongst many 'pools' punters', the Scottish matches nearly always provide a couple of score-draws.

However, the choice of divisions is yours, but I cannot stress too strongly that once having made it, **stick to it** through thick and thin. Be happy in the knowledge that although your combination won't come up 'trumps' every week, it will include about 80% of the score-draws several times throughout the season.

Furthermore, all is not lost on the many occasions when the most fruitful three leagues are not those you have selected, because when there is a surfeit of score-draws, say 14 or 15, then several combinations, of which yours may be one, will include 8, 9 or even 10 of the 3-pointers.

Granted that even if you win a first dividend on one of these weeks it won't be a fortune, but it is very rewarding and satisfying to get 24 points however small the prize. But I'll stress again, stick to the same leagues throughout the season, and when possible always remember the adage 'Never change horses in midstream'.

Having made your final choice (or choices should you decide on using more than one combination of three divisions), the number of matches – of which there will be about 33 or 34, will have to be pruned in accordance with the number of selections you ultimately decide to include in your entry. Ideally, the fewer left out the better, bearing in mind that every match is a potential score-draw. However, a full-cover block perm covering 32 matches is very expensive, but well worthwhile in the case of syndicates.

In the next chapter I describe and illustrate full-cover block perms covering from 14 to 32 selections at a fraction of the cost of orthodox full cover perms. Checking charts are not required, because as I've said, every block-perm provides full cover each block. In order to make doubly sure that readers understand the instructions and also to illustrate the ease with which the entry can be checked, each individual block perm includes a facsimile coupon entry together with hypothetical results which can be checked against the block perm.

Readers will find that in every case the illustrated examples include a winning line containing 24 points. The cost of entry for each of the three major pools firms is given to the nearest penny (at the current cost per line, i.e. 1989-90 season).

Incidentally the 'three leagues' system does not apply to the Australian Summer Pools, the score-draw pattern of which is not only entirely inconsistent, but the form of individual teams is infinitely more unpredictable than that of their English, Scottish and Welsh counterparts.

In fact this is a case for quoting the Chinese proverb 'An ounce of luck is more valuable than a pound of knowledge'. Never was there a greater truism in any walk of life, let along in trying to weigh up Australian form.

I can offer no advice therefore on the pinpointing of score-draws; it is a matter of 'you pays your money and takes your choice'. Nevertheless, having made your selections, I most strongly advocate using one of the 'perms' described and illustrated in the following pages, because should you be clairvoyant enough to be successful in pin-pointing the score-draws, it would be a pity to waste them on any other than a full-cover block perm.

Each of the following permutations provide **full cover** for each block (or column). If you have 8 score-draws in the requisite blocks (or columns) then YOU MUST HAVE 24 POINTS. But avoid duplicating any of your selections otherwise the entry may be void!

In the 'results' column, 1 denotes a 'Home Win' (1 point), 1½ an 'Away Win' (1½ points), 2 a 'No Score Draw' (2 points), and 3 denotes a 'Score Draw' (3 points).

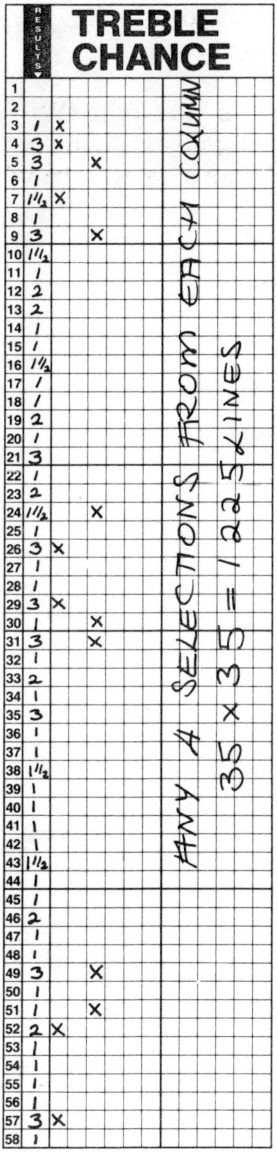

14 SELECTIONS

By far the best method of dealing with 14 matches is to divide them up into two columns with 7 in each – because 4 correct forecasts in each 7 is the most likely ratio they will fall should you select 8 score-draws.

After all, readers must be only too aware from their own past experiences that whereas 4 correct out of seven selections is exceptionally good picking, the chances of 5, 6 or 7 being correct are so remote that they can be virtually discarded.

It is on this same principal that I advocate full-cover-blocks (or columns) for all the ensuing perms.

So in this particular case, select 14 matches in two columns with 7 in each. Any 4 correct in each column will give you 24 points.

Write alongside your entry:

Any 4 selections from each column.

35 × 35 = 1,225 lines.

This is a vast saving on a full orthodox perm which requires 3,003 lines, and the cost is:

Zetters – 82p

Vernons – £2.73

Littlewoods – £10.89

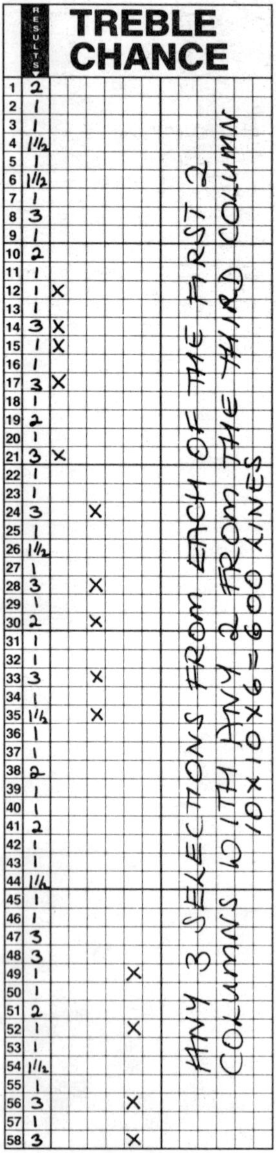

14 SELECTIONS

A very economical method, and one ideal for the housewife who likes her weekly flutter on the lower-stake pool, is to divide your selections into 3 columns, with 5 in each of the first 2, and 4 in the third.

Any 3 correct forecasts in each of the first 2 columns with 2 correct in the third wins 1st dividend.

Write alongside your entry:

Any 3 selections from each of the first 2 columns with any 2 from the third.

10 × 10 × 6 = 600 lines.

Cost:

Zetters – 40p

Vernons – £1.34

Littlewoods – £5.34

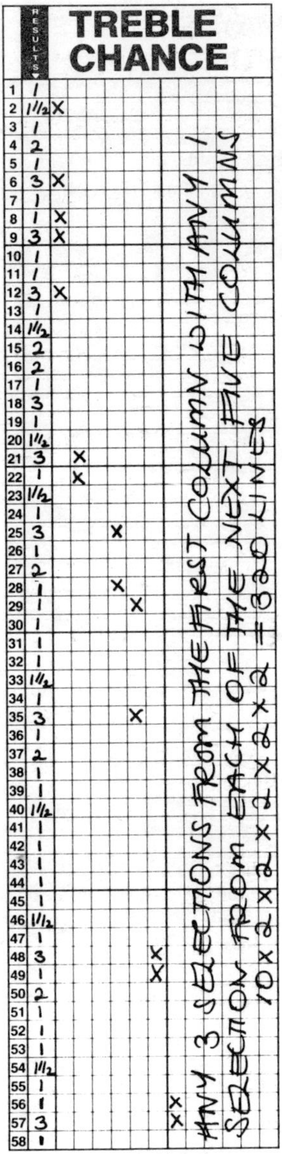

15 SELECTIONS

The success of this little 15-match permutation is dependent on forecasting 3 score-draws in your first 5 selections. Having achieved this objective however, then a first dividend is 'well on the cards'.

Simply divide your 15 selections by entering the first 5 in the first column, then mark off 2 matches in each of the ensuing five columns. Should you manage to find 3 score-draws in your first column, then the road to a 'first' is all down hill, because just one correct forecast in each of the remaining columns makes you a candidate for sending off a telephone claim. Having entered your selections on the coupon as instructed, write alongside:

Any 3 selections from the first column with any 1 selection from each of the next five columns.

10 × 2 × 2 × 2 × 2 × 2 = 320 lines.

Cost:

Zetters – 22p*

Vernons – 72p

Littlewoods – £2.85

*Zetters investors please note that this perm costs less than their minimum coupon stake (25p). I suggest either making 2 separate entries, or better still, turn to page 61 where 20 matches are covered for 43p.

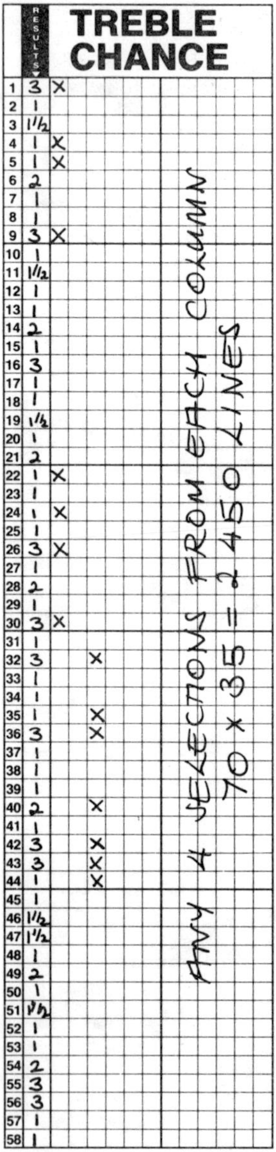

15 SELECTIONS

Divide selections into 2 columns with 8 in one and 7 in the other. Any 4 correct in each column scores 24 points.

Write alongside your entry:

Any 4 selections from each column.

70 × 35 = 2,450 lines.

Again this full-cover-block perm represents a considerable saving on a full orthodox perm which would require 6,435 lines.

Cost:

Zetters – £1.64

Vernons – £5.45

Littlewoods – £21.78

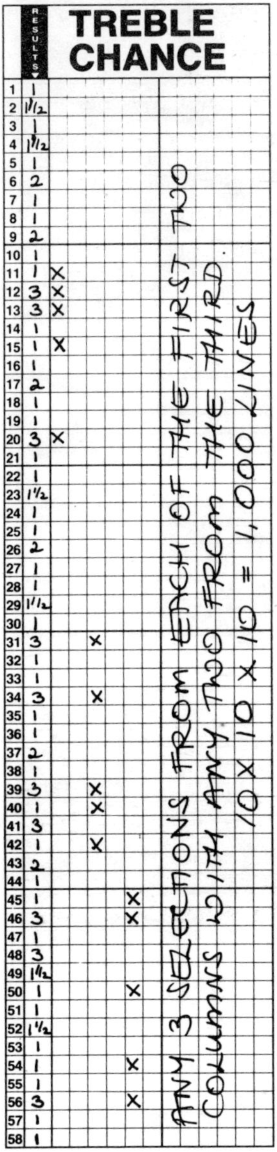

15 SELECTIONS

For the housewives little flutter I recommend the following full-cover-block perm.

Divide your selections into three separate columns, with 5 in each.

Any 3 correct in each of the first 2 columns with any 2 correct in the third wins 24 points.

Write alongside your 3 columns:

Any 3 selections from each of the first 2 columns with any 2 from the third.

10 × 10 × 10 = 1,000 lines.

Cost:

Zetters – 67p

Vernons – £2.23

Littlewoods – £8.89

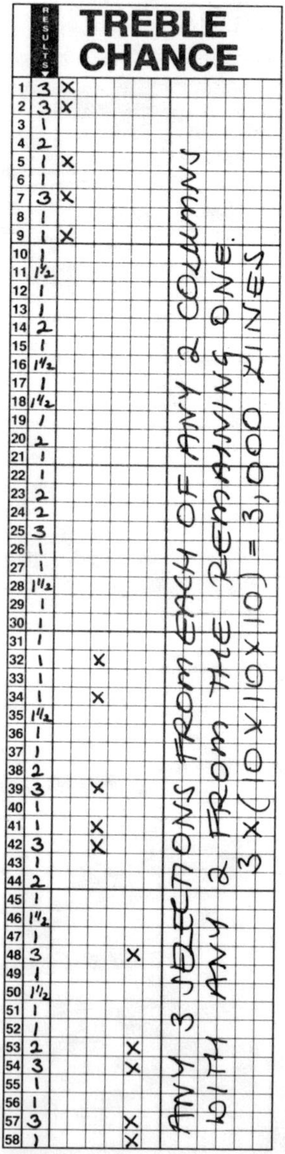

15 SELECTIONS

An elaboration of the water-tight 3-block perm on the previous page is to cover fully the eventuality of 3 score-draws falling in ANY 2 of the 3 columns with 2 falling in the remaining one. Simply fill in your 15 selections in three separate columns of 5 in each and write alongside:

Any 3 selections from each of any 2 columns with any 2 from the remaining one.

3 × (10 × 10 × 10) = 3,000 lines.

Cost:

Zetters – £2.00

Vernons – £6.67

Littlewoods – £26.67

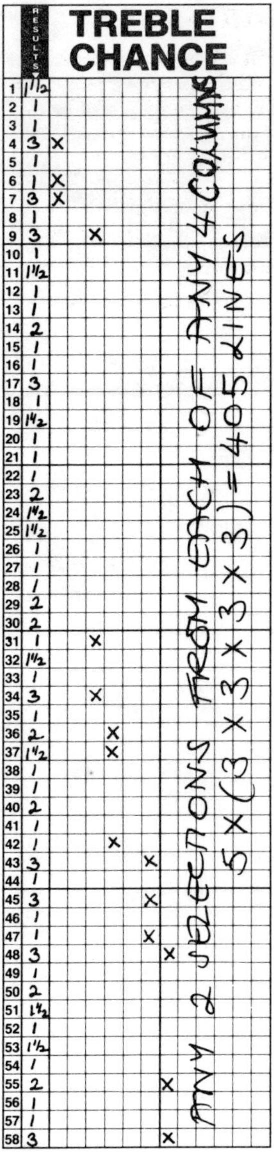

15 SELECTIONS

The following 405-line full cover-block perm will give you a very good run for your money for a comparative small outlay, and is the answer for the housewife who may have run a little short on the housekeeping – the cost being less than that of a couple of postage stamps (on the lowest stake pool.)

Divide the 15 selections into five columns with 3 in each.

Any 2 correct forecasts in each of any 4 columns wins 1st dividend. Write alongside your five columns:

Any 2 selections from each of any four columns.

5 × (3 × 3 × 3 × 3) = 405 lines.

Cost:

Zetters – 27p

Vernons – 90p

Littlewoods – £3.60

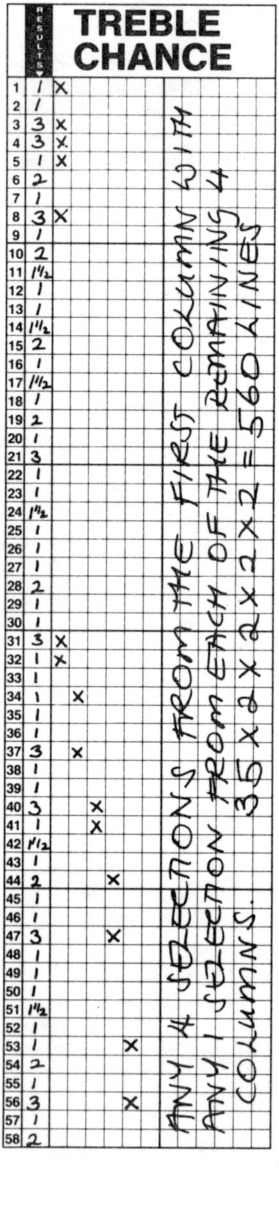

15 SELECTIONS

The following full-cover block perm should give investors a good run for their money at a cost which is well within the purse-strings of everyone.

Mark off your selections in five columns, with 7 in the first and 2 in each of the other four.

To score maximum points you must have 4 correct forecasts in the first column with just 1 correct in each of the remaining four columns.

Write alongside your entry:

Any 4 selections from the first column with any 1 selection from each of the remaining four columns.

35 × 2 × 2 × 2 × 2 = 560 lines.

Cost:

Zetters – 38p

Vernons – £1.25

Littlewoods – £4.98

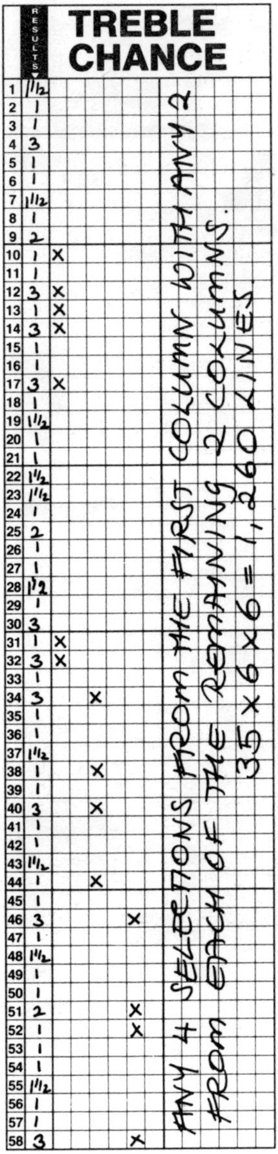

15 SELECTIONS

My final method of covering 15 matches and one which should occasionally cause a quickening of the pulse at 'Pools checking time', is to divide your selections into three columns, with 7 in the first and 4 in each of the remaining two.

Any 4 correct in the first column wih any 2 correct in each of the other two scores maximum points.

Write alongside your entry:

Any 4 selections from the first column with any 2 from each of the remaining two columns.

35 × 6 × 6 = 1,260 lines.

Cost:

Zetters – 84p

Vernons – £2.80

Littlewoods – £11.20

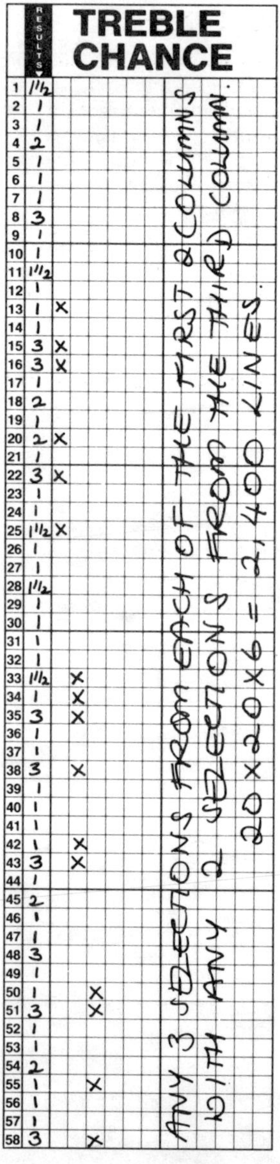

16 SELECTIONS

Both the newspaper pools correspondents and the pools companies themselves base a very high proportion of their 'plans' on 16 selections. Apart from an orthodox full perm which requires 12,870 lines, my 2,400 line full-cover 3-block method must rank as a clear favourite in covering almost a third of the coupon list.

Each block (or column) allows for a 50% error in forecasting, and at less than one fifth the cost of an ordinary full perm represents extremely good value for money whilst at the same time affording a very realistic chance of a 1st dividend should your forecasting be reasonably accurate.

Having decided on your selections, mark them off in three columns with 6 in each of the first two and the remaining 4 matches in the third column.

Then write alongside your entry:

Any 3 selections from each of the first 2 columns with any 2 selections from the third column.

20 × 20 × 6 = 2,400 lines.

Cost:

Zetters – £1.60

Vernons – £5.34

Littlewoods – £21.34

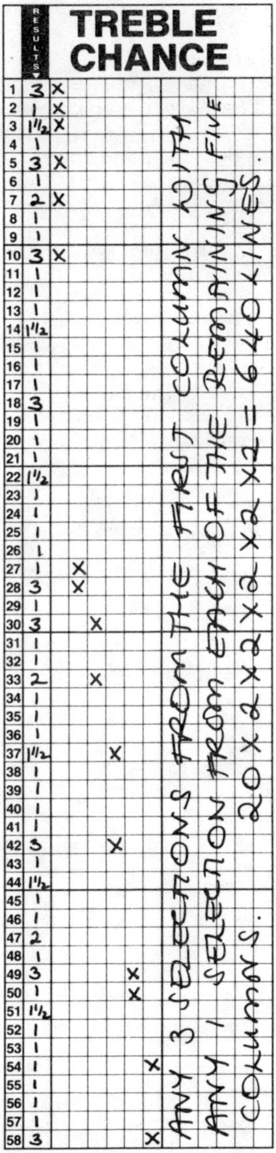

16 SELECTIONS

Even allowing for half your selections being wrong, the following full-cover block perm could prove a certain dividend winner – especially should 'Dame Fortune' be guiding your writing-hand when marking off your 16 potential score-draws. Furthermore, the cost is well within everyone's range.

Enter your first 6 selections in the first column, then mark off 2 in each of the next five columns making up your 16 matches.

Any 3 correct in the first column with just 1 correct in each of the other five columns wins a 'first' plus multiple minor dividends.

Write alongside your entry:

Any 3 selections from the first column with any 1 selection from each of the remaining five columns.

20 × 2 × 2 × 2 × 2 × 2 = 640 lines.

Cost:

Zetters – 43p

Vernons – £1.43

Littlewoods – £5.69

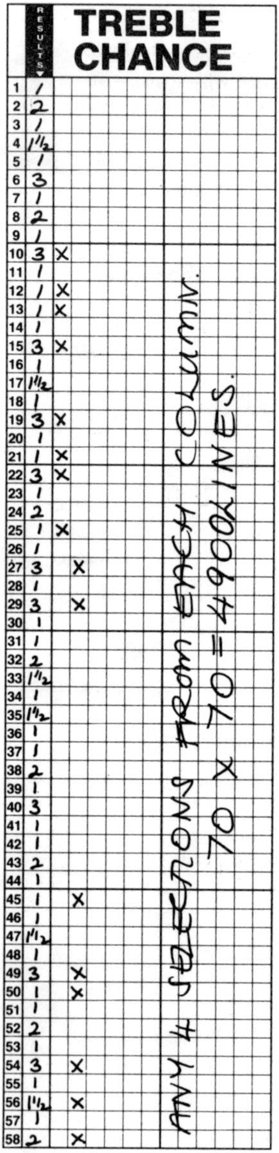

16 SELECTIONS

Full orthodox permutations involving 16 matches and less are well within the scope of both individuals and syndicates. Nevertheless, because of the wastage of lines (referred to on page •), full-cover block perms at only a fraction the cost are of infinitely better value.

An ordinary full-perm covering 16 selections would require 12,870 lines, but by dividing the matches into two columns with 8 in each, and taking ANY 4 from each, it can be done with just 4,900 lines.

So mark off 8 selections in each of two columns – if you have 4 correct forecasts in each then you are a winner.

Just write alongside your entry:

Any 4 selections from each column.

70 × 70 = 4,900 lines.

Cost:

Zetters – £3.27

Vernons – £10.89

Littlewoods – £43.56

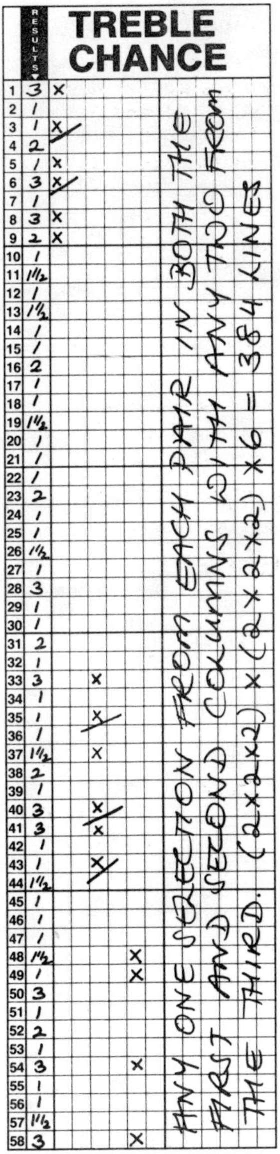

16 SELECTIONS

This method provides full-cover each section at a cost which practically everyone can afford on whichever of the major pools they patronise.

Divide your selections into three columns with 6 in each of the first two and 4 in the third.

Then divide each of the first two columns selections into pairs with a firm dividing line under the 2nd and 4th match, so that you have 3 separate pairs in each of the first two columns.

Any 1 selection correct in each pair from both the first two columns with any 2 correct out of the 4 in the third column wins 1st dividend.

Write alongside your three columns:

1 selection from each pair in both the first and second columns with any 2 from the third.

$(2 \times 2 \times 2) \times (2 \times 2 \times 2) \times 6 = 384$ lines.

Cost:

Zetters – 26p

Vernons – 86p

Littlewoods – £3.42

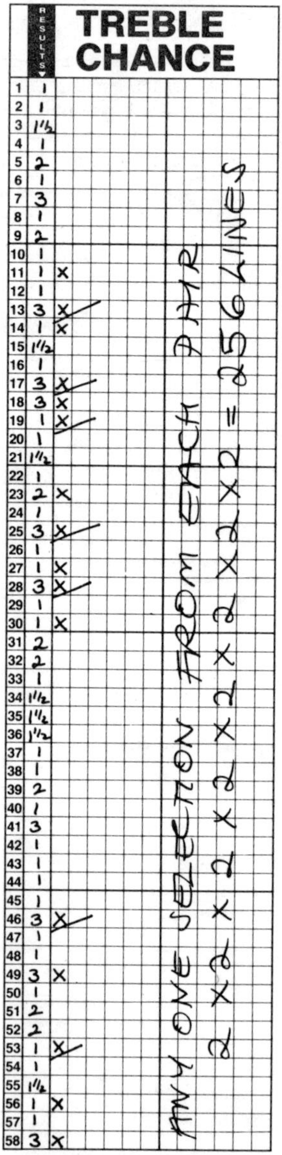

16 SELECTIONS

An excellent little 'housewives' entry, and one which again gives full cover each section, yet allows for 50% error in selection is entered as follows:

Mark off your 16 selections in one column with a dividing line under the 2nd, 4th, 6th, 8th, 10th, 12th and 14th selection, giving you eight pairs.

Either 1 correct in each pair will give you 24 points.

Write alongside your selections:

Any 1 selection from each pair.

$2 \times 2 \times 2 \times 2 \times 2 \times 2 \times 2 \times 2 = 256$ lines.

As the cost of this method on Zetters is less than their minimum stake of 25p, I suggest having 2 attempts.

Cost:

Zetters – 17p

Vernons – 57p

Littlewoods – £2.28

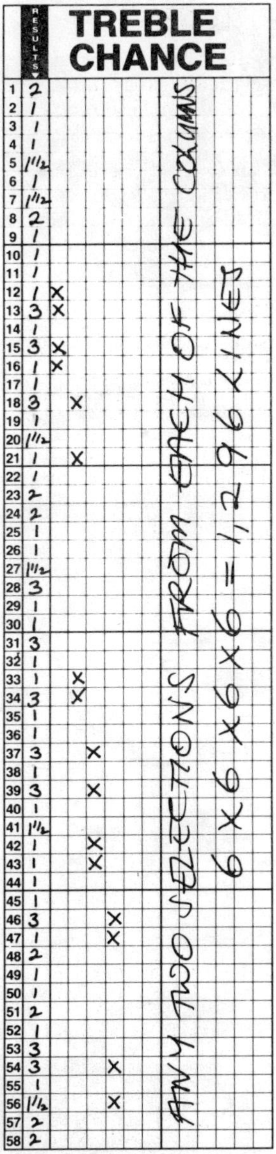

16 SELECTIONS

Another first-class way of dealing with 16 matches, and one which gives plenty of scope for error but at the same time provides full-cover in every column, is to divide your selections into four columns with 4 in each.

Any 2 correct in each column and you have 24 points.

Write alongside your entry:

Any 2 selections from each column.

6 × 6 × 6 × 6 = 1,296 lines.

Cost:

Zetters – 87p

Vernons – £2.88

Littlewoods – £11.52

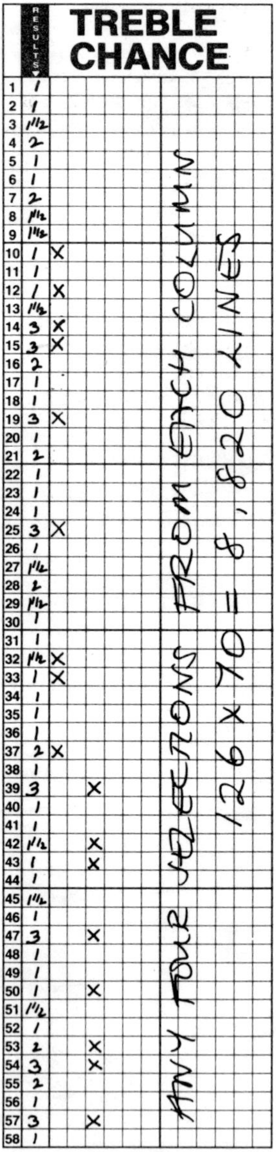

17 SELECTIONS

Two full-cover columns is the soundest way to cover 17 matches – and at 8,820 lines cost fractionally over a third that of a full orthodox perm.

Simply mark off 9 selections in one column and 8 in the other. Any 4 correct in each column and you have a 1st dividend.

Write alongside the entry:

Any 4 selections from each column.

126 × 70 = 8,820 lines.

Whereas an ordinary full perm (which I wouldn't recommend anyway) would be far too expensive for the individual or families who like to 'club together', this method could be within that 'price bracket' on the lower stake pools.

Cost:

Zetters – £5.88

Vernons – £19.60

Littlewoods – £78.40

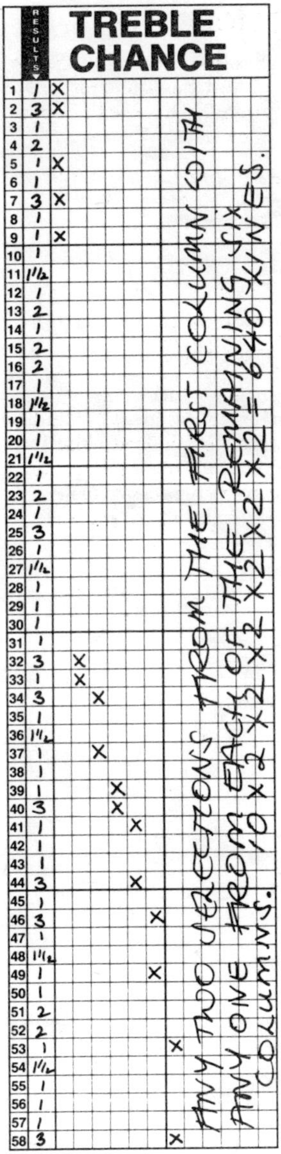

17 SELECTIONS

A method which will not stretch the financial resources of anyone on the lower stake pools, and one which more often than not should provide you with a solid foundation for 'Scooping the Pool', is to divide the matches selected into 7 columns.

In the first one select 5, and in the remaining six columns enter 2 selections in each.

To win a 1st dividend you must have 2 correct forecasts in the first column (with 5 matches to choose from this shouldn't prove too difficult), and 1 correct in each of the other six columns.

Write alongside your seven columns:

Any 2 selections from the first column with any 1 from each of the remaining six columns.

10 × 2 × 2 × 2 × 2 × 2 × 2 = 640 lines.

Cost:

Zetters – 43p

Vernons – £1.43

Littlewoods – £5.69

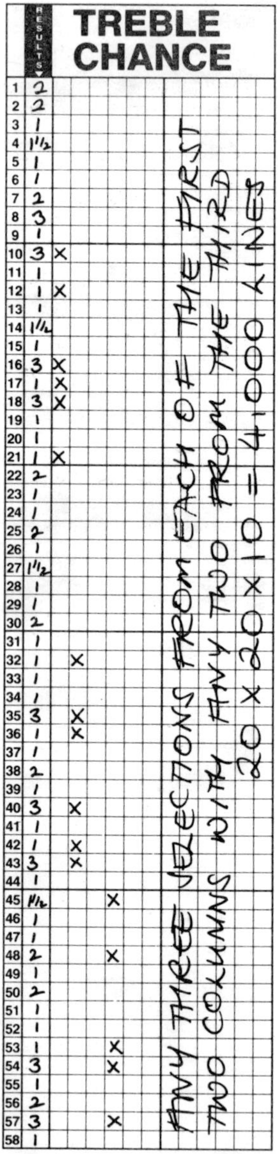

17 SELECTIONS

Another first-class way to deal with this number of matches is to divide your selections into three columns with 6 in each of the first two and 5 in the third.

Any 3 correct forecasts in each of the first two columns with 2 in the third, and you win 1st dividend.

Write alongside your entry:

Any 3 selections from each of the first two columns with any 2 from the third.

20 × 20 × 10 = 4,000 lines.

This full-cover block perm is ideal for the individual investor on the lowest stake pool, but well worthy of forming syndicates (or making into a joint family effort) on the bigger stake pools.

Cost:

Zetters – £2.67

Vernons – £8.89

Littlewoods – £35.54

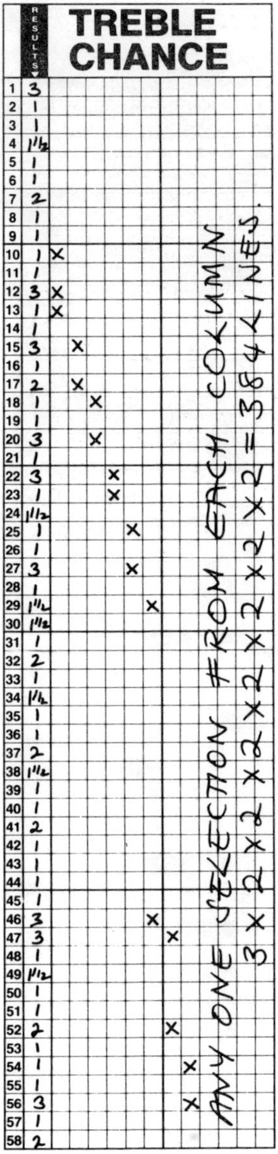

17 SELECTIONS

The most economical way to cover 17 selections, but at the same time one which will make a serious check of your coupon on a Saturday evening well worthwhile on occasions is the following:

Divide your selections into eight columns with 3 in the first, and 2 in each of the other seven.

1 correct forecast in each column will win 1st dividend.

Just write alongside the eight columns:

Any 1 selection from each column.

$3 \times 2 \times 2 \times 2 \times 2 \times 2 \times 2 \times 2 = 384$ lines.

Bearing in mind the number of lines required for a full orthodox perm (24,310), this represents 'value for money'.

Cost:

Zetters – 26p

Vernons – 86p

Littlewoods – £3.42

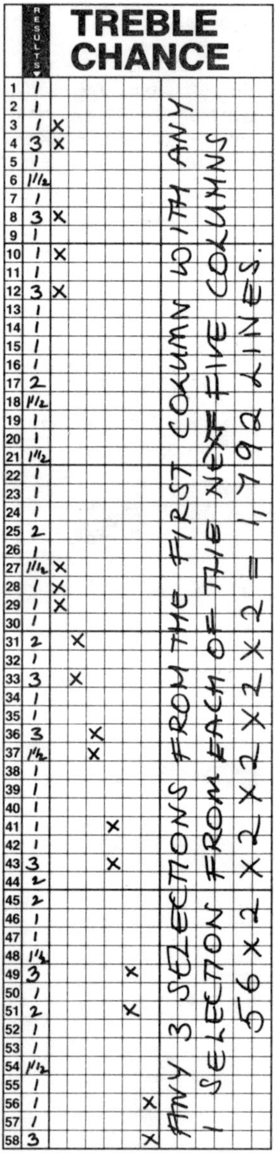

18 SELECTIONS

Many punters will frequently get off to a 'flyer' with this permutation because for starters you have 8 selections from which to find your first 3 score-draws and so build a solid foundation for landing that elusive 'Jackpot'.

Furthermore, the cost is well within the range of most Zetters and Vernons punters whlst those opting for Littlewoods may find it well worthwhile clubbing together with family and friends in order to participate in what could prove to be a 'financial bonanza'.

Enter the first 8 selections in one column, then mark off 2 selections in each of the next five columns. 3 score-draws in the first column with 1 in each of the other five columns wins a first dividend together with multiple minor ones.

Write alongside your entry:

Any 3 selections from the first column with any 1 selection from each of the next five columns.

56 × 2 × 2 × 2 × 2 × 2 = 1,792 lines.

Cost:

Zetters – £1.20

Vernons – £3.99

Littlewoods – £15.93

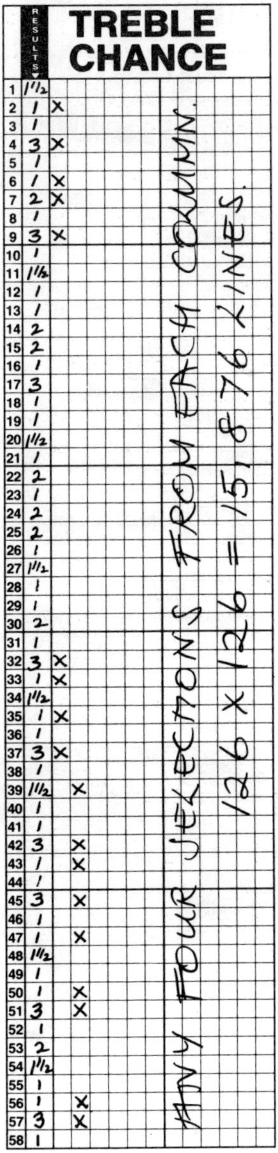

18 SELECTIONS

The most effective (but unfortunately expensive) method of covering almost a third of the matches on the coupon is to divide your selections into two columns with 9 in each.

Any 4 correct in each column wins first prize.

Just write alongside the entry:

Any 4 selections from each column.

126 × 126 = 15,876 lines.

This Full-Cover-Block perm costs just a litle over a third that of an ordinary ‘full perm’, and is ideal for large sydicates.

Cost:

Zetters – £10.59

Vernons – £35.28

Littlewoods – £141.02

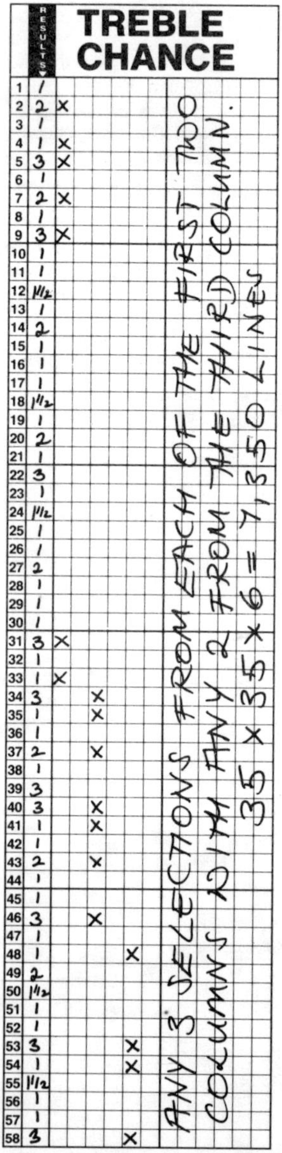

18 SELECTIONS

A less expensive, but nevertheless very sound way to deal with 18 matches is to divide your selections into three columns with 7 in each of the first two and 4 in the third.

3 correct forecasts in each of the first two columns with 2 correct in the third will produce 24 points.

Write alongside your entry:

Any 3 selections from each of the first two columns with any 2 from the third.

35 × 35 × 6 = 7,350 lines.

On the lowest-stake pool, if beyond the resources of the individual, this first-class water-tight perm is well worth pooling resources with family or friends. In the case of the other pools firms, forming a syndicate is the answer.

Cost:

Zetters – £4.90

Vernons – £16.34

Littlewoods – £65.34

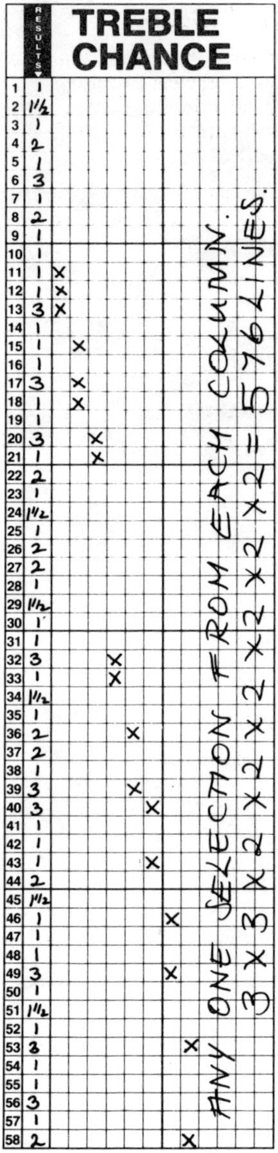

18 SELECTIONS

I thoroughly recommend the following method of dealing with 18 selections, because not only does it fall within the 'financial compass' of everyone, but also allows lots of scope for error – whilst still providing 'full-cover-each-column'.

Divide your selections into eight columns with 3 in each of the first two, and 2 in each of the remaining six (making 18 in total). Any 1 correct in each column will produce 24 points.

Write alongside your eight columns:

Any 1 selection from each column.

$3 \times 3 \times 2 \times 2 \times 2 \times 2 \times 2 \times 2 = 576$ lines.

Cost:

Zetters – 39p

Vernons – £1.28

Littlewoods – £5.12

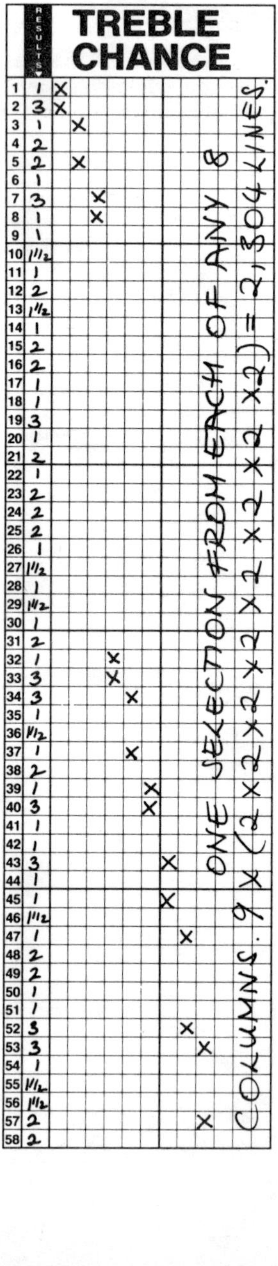

18 SELECTIONS

The following method, which is well within the 'purse range' of most individual investors on the lower stake pool, but will certainly necessitate a joint effort on the '8/9p per line' pool, provides as usual full cover each column, and is sure to give rise to excitement at 'pools checking time' more than once throughout the season.

Mark off 2 selections in each of nine columns.

1 correct in each of ANY eight of the columns will produce 24 points.

Write alongside the entry:

1 selection from each of any eight columns.

9 × (2 × 2 × 2 × 2 × 2 × 2 × 2 × 2) = 2,304 lines.

Cost:

Zetters – £1.54

Vernons – £5.12

Littlewoods – £20.48

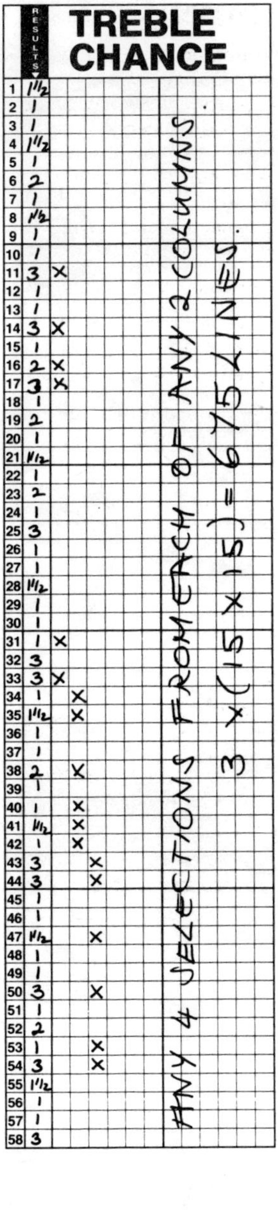

18 SELECTIONS

A very economical full-cover-block perm which should appeal to a lot of investors, can be achieved with only 675 lines.

Divide your 18 selections into three columns with 6 in each. Any 4 correct forecasts in each of any two columns wins 1st dividend.

Write alongside your entry:

Any 4 selections from each of any two columns.

3 × (15 × 15) = 675 lines.

Cost:

Zetters – 45p

Vernons – £1.50

Littlewoods – £6.00

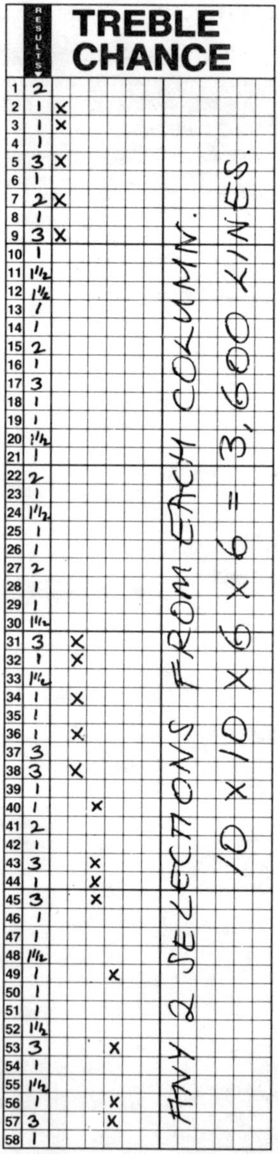

18 SELECTIONS

I thoroughly recommend the following method which gives full block cover with a mere 3,600 lines as compared with a full orthodox perm which requires 43,758 lines.

If the purse-strings or wallet will not stretch to the cost of this perm it is well worth-while clubbing together with friends or family and forming a small syndicate.

Simply divide your 18 selections into four columns, with 5 in each of the first two and 4 in each of the other two.

Any 2 correct forecasts in each column and you win 1st dividend.

Write alongside your entry:

Any 2 selections from each column.

10 × 10 × 6 × 6 = 3,600 lines.

Cost:

Zetters – £2.40

Vernons – £8.00

Littlewoods – £32.00

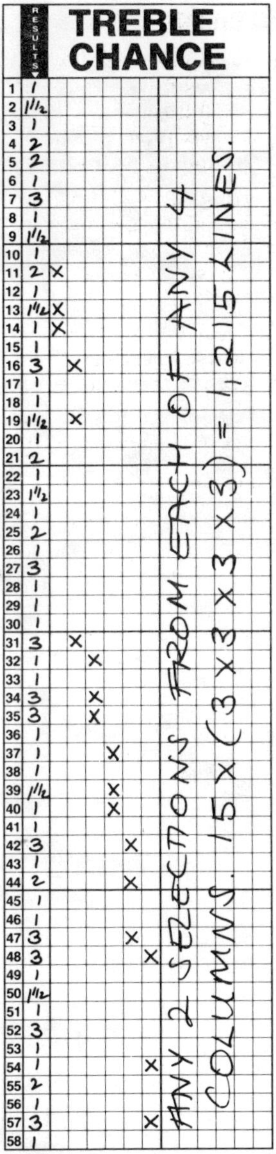

18 SELECTIONS

Another very effective way of covering 18 selections at a cost most individuals can afford on the lower-stake Pools, but which is well-worth the forming of a small syndicate on the $^{8}/_{9}$p a line pool, is to divide your selections into six columns with 3 selections in each.

Any 2 correct forecasts in each of any four columns will produce 24 points.

Write alongside your entry:

Any 2 selections from each of any four columns.

15 × (3 × 3 × 3 × 3) = 1,215 lines.

Cost:

Zetters – 81p

Vernons – £2.70

Littlewoods – £10.80

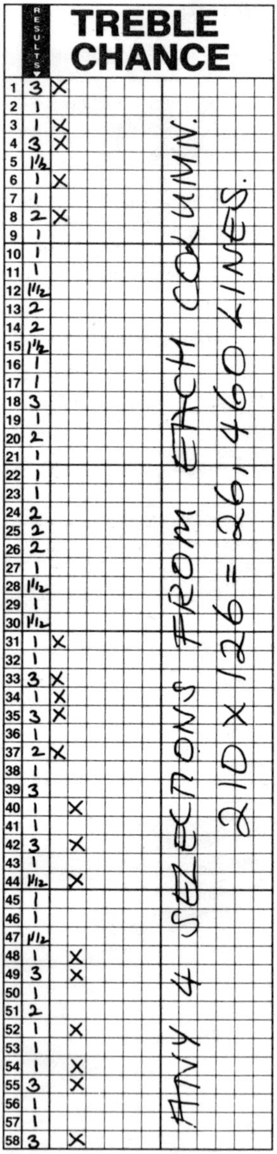

19 SELECTIONS

A full orthodox perm to cover 19 matches requires 75,582 lines – which is obviously beyond the means of even the large syndicates. However, the following full-cover-block method is certain to produce results at a fraction of the cost, and is certainly a realistic proposition for syndicates on the lower-stake pools.

Divide your selections into two columns with 10 in the first and 9 in the second.

All you need to win a first dividend is 4 correct forecasts in each column.

Write alongside the two columns:

Any 4 selections from each column.

210 × 126 = 26,460 lines.

Cost:

Zetters – £17.64

Vernons – £58.80

Littlewoods – £235.20

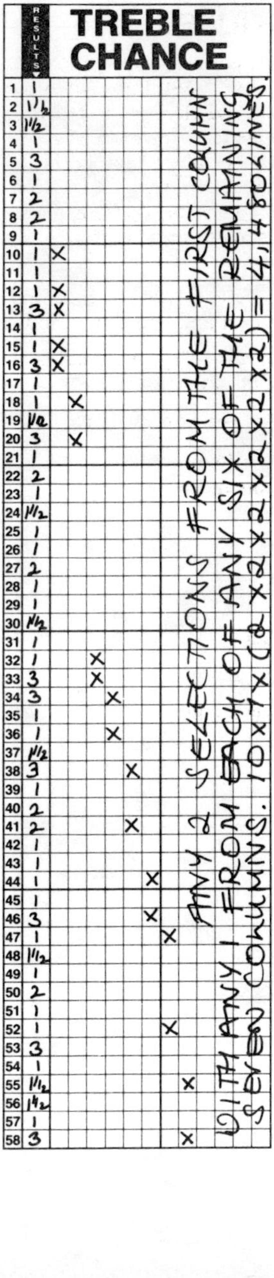

19 SELECTIONS

An inexpensive way of dealing with 19 selections and which should appeal to many of my readers is as follows:

Divide them into eight columns with 5 selections in the first and 2 in each of the remaining seven (totalling 19).

To win 1st dividend you must have 2 correct forecasts in your first column with 1 correct in each of any six of the remaining seven columns.

Write alongside your entry:

Any 2 selections from the first column with any 1 from each of any six of the remaining seven columns.

$10 \times 7 \times (2 \times 2 \times 2 \times 2 \times 2 \times 2) =$ 4,480 lines.

Whereas some individuals will be able to afford the outlay to do this perm on the lower stake pools, others who find it too expensive would find it well worth the effort of 'clubbing together' with friends, or forming a small syndicate.

Cost:

Zetters – £2.99

Vernons – £9.96

Littlewoods – £39.83

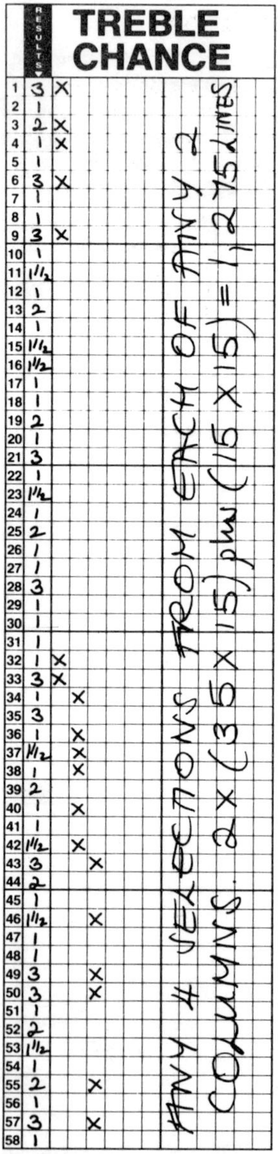

19 SELECTIONS

A very economical method of dealing with 19 matches and one which should cause a quickening of the heartbeat occasionally at 'pools-checking-time' is the following:

Divide your selections into three columns with 7 in the first and 6 in each of the other two.

4 score-draws in each of any two columns will win you a first dividend.

Just write alongside your three columns:

Any 4 selections from each of any two columns.

2 × (35 × 15) plus (15 × 15) = 1,275 lines.

Cost:

Zetters – 85p

Vernons – £2.84

Littlewoods – £11.34

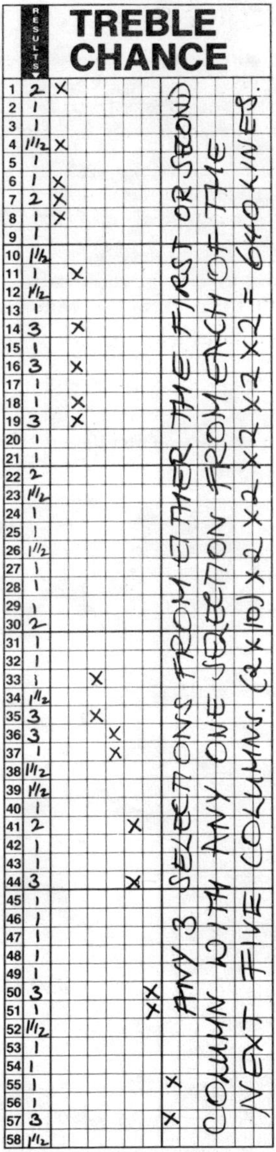

20 SELECTIONS

For investors who like a lot for their money, this permutation represents very good value indeed, and is certain to reap a rich harvest on some occasions – providing there are 3 score-draws in either of the first two columns.

To enter, mark off 5 selections in each of the first two columns and 2 selections in each of the next five columns.

Write alongside your entry:

Any 3 selections from either the first or second column with any 1 selection from each of the next five columns.

$(2 \times 10) \times 2 \times 2 \times 2 \times 2 \times 2 = 640$ lines.

Cost:

Zetters – 43p

Vernons – £1.43

Littlewoods – £5.69

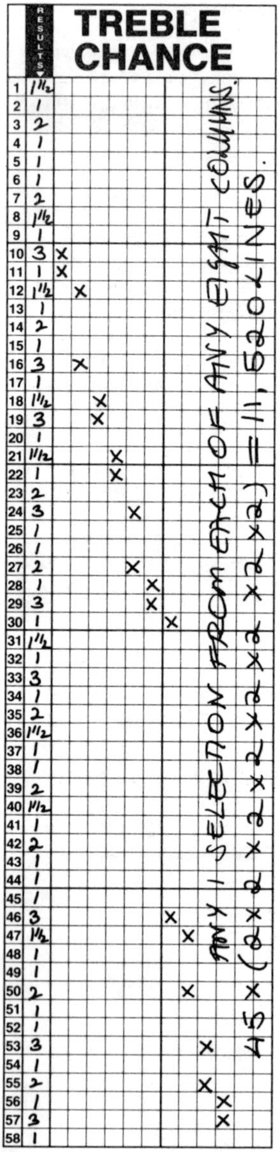

20 SELECTIONS

There is no really cheap yet at the same time reliable way of covering 20 matches.

On the other hand, using this number (and upwards) of selections provides a realistic chance of pin-pointing 8 score-draws reasonably often.

So I have included a fairly wide range of full-cover block perms, the least expensive of which are well within the range of some individuals and families who may think it worthwhile to pool their resources.

The following will undoubtedly appeal to this category and syndicates on the lower stakes pools.

Divide your selections into 10 columns with 2 selections in each. Any 1 correct forecast in each of ANY 8 columns will win 1st dividend.

Write alongside your ten columns:

Any 1 selection from each of any eight columns.

$45 \times (2 \times 2 \times 2 \times 2 \times 2 \times 2 \times 2 \times 2)$
$= 11{,}520$ lines.

Cost:

Zetters – £7.68

Vernons – £25.60

Littlewoods – £102.40

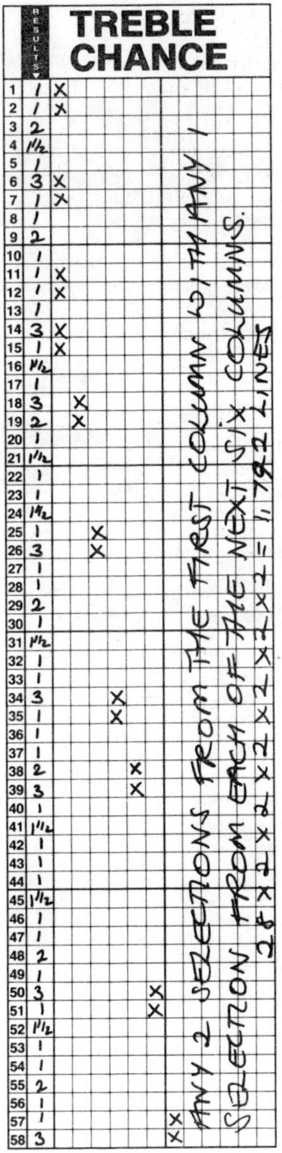

20 SELECTIONS

Disciples of this 1,792-line perm will often find their hearts a-fluttering at 'pools-checking' time, because more often than not they will succeed in 'netting' the 2 score-draws required from their first 8 selections to set them on the road to a possible fortune.

Furthermore, this 7-column 'gem' of a perm is comparatively inexpensive when one considers that an orthodox full-permutation covering 20 matches would require 125,970 lines – or in monetary terms £83.98 on Zetters, £279.94 on Vernons and on Littlewoods you'd need over a 'GRAND' – £1,119.74 to be exact.

So to 'set your stall out', enter your first 8 selections in the first column and 2 selections in each of the next six columns. Any 2 correct in the first column with one correct in each of the next 6 columns will secure that coveted 24 points.

Write alongside your entry:

Any 2 selections from the first column with any 1 selection from each of the next six columns.

28 × 2 × 2 × 2 × 2 × 2 × 2 = 1,792 lines.

Cost:

Zetters – £1.20

Vernons – £3.99

Littlewoods – £15.93

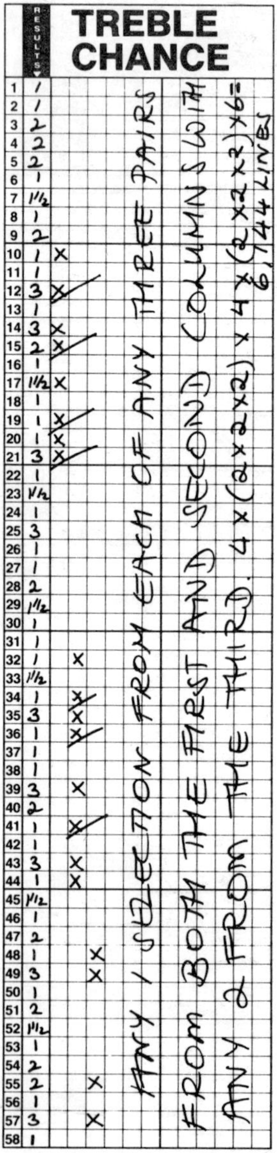

20 SELECTIONS

The following method will undoubtedly appeal to both individuals on the lowest-stake pool and syndicates on the others.

At a moderate cost it offers a realistic chance of being amongst the 1st dividend winners.

Divide your selections into three columns with 8 in each of the first two and 4 in the third. Then divide each column of 8 matches into pairs with a dividing line under the 2nd, 4th and 6th selection, (so that your first two columns will each consist of 4 pairs).

Any 1 selection from each of any three pairs in each of the first two columns with any 2 correct out of the 4 selections in the third column wins 1st dividend.

Write clearly alongside your entry:

Any 1 selection from each of any three pairs, from both the first and second columns with any 2 from the third.

$4 \times (2 \times 2 \times 2) \times 4 \times (2 \times 2 \times 2) \times 6 = 6{,}144$ lines.

Cost:

Zetters – £4.01

Vernons – £13.66

Littlewoods – £54.62

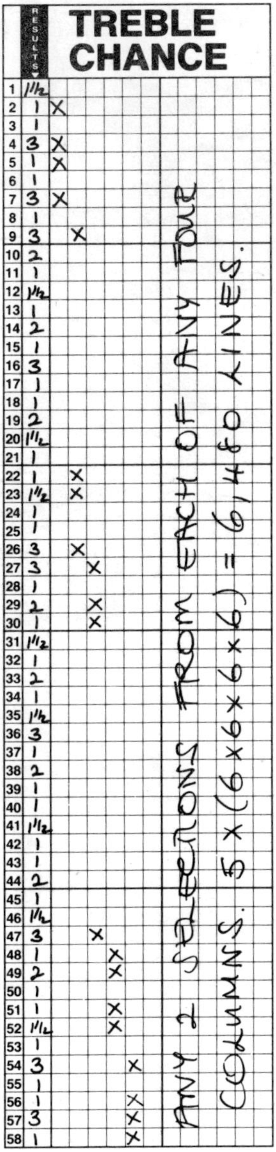

20 SELECTIONS

A really first-class way of covering a score of matches, and one which again may necessitate families pooling their resources on the low stake pool (or forming a syndicate on the other pools), is to divide your selections into five columns with 4 in each.

Any 2 correct forecasts in each of any four columns will win 1st dividend with 24 points.

Write alongside your entry:

Any 2 selections from each of any four columns.

5 × (6 × 6 × 6 × 6) = 6,480 lines.

Cost:

Zetters – £4.32

Vernons – £14.40

Littlewoods – £57.60

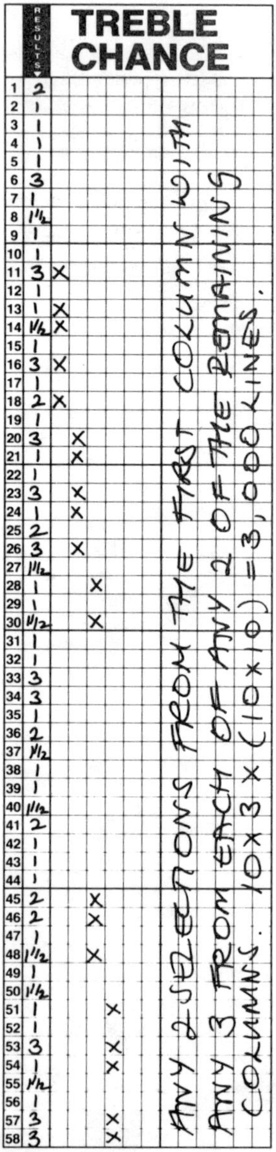

20 SELECTIONS

The most economical way I can suggest to cover this number of matches, and one which will make a serious check of the coupon well worthwhile occasionally, is to divide your selections into four columns with 5 in each.

In order to score 24 points you must have 2 score-draws in the first column with 3 correct in each of any two of the remaining three columns.

Write alongside your entry:

Any 2 selections from the first column with any 3 from each of any two of the remaining columns.

$10 \times 3 \times (10 \times 10) = 3{,}000$ lines.

Cost:

Zetters – £2.00

Vernons – £6.67

Littlewoods – £26.67

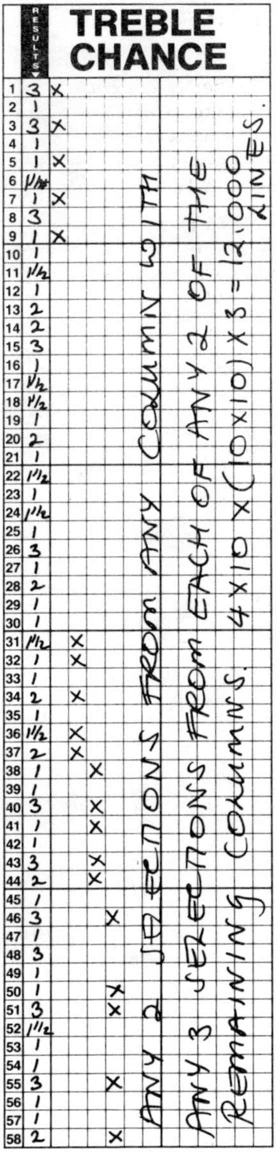

20 SELECTIONS

An improvisation of the 3,000 line method described on the previous page allows for 2 score-draws falling in ANY of the four columns each of which contains 5 selections, with 3 in any two of the remaining three. This way is ideally suited to syndicates. So mark off 5 selections in each of four columns and write alongside:

Any 2 selections from any column with any 3 selections from each of any 2 of the remaining columns.

$4 \times 10 \times (10 \times 10) \times 3 = 12{,}000$ lines.

Cost:

Zetters – £8.00

Vernons – £26.67

Littlewoods – £106.67

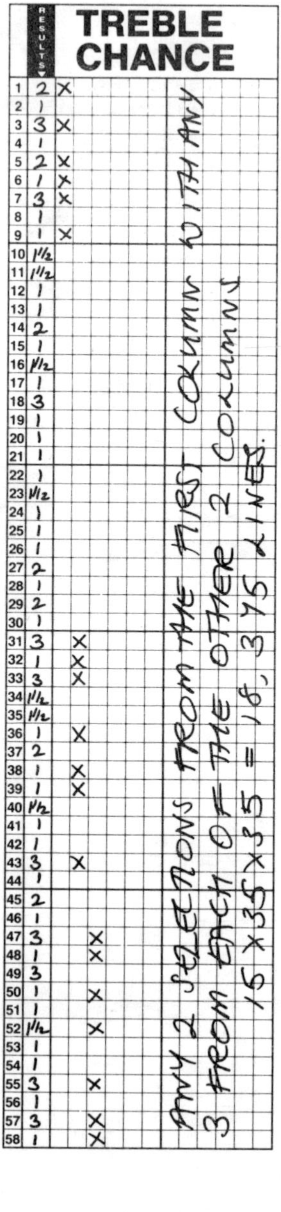

20 SELECTIONS

The following should appeal to syndicates on the lower-stake pools. Divide your selections into three columns, the first containing 6 selections, with 7 in each of the other two.

Any 2 correct forecasts in the first column with any 3 correct in each of the other two wins first dividend.

Write alongside the three columns:

Any 2 selections from the first column with any 3 from each of the other two columns.

15 × 35 × 35 = 18,375 lines.

Cost:

Zetters – £12.25

Vernons – £40.84

Littlewoods – £163.34

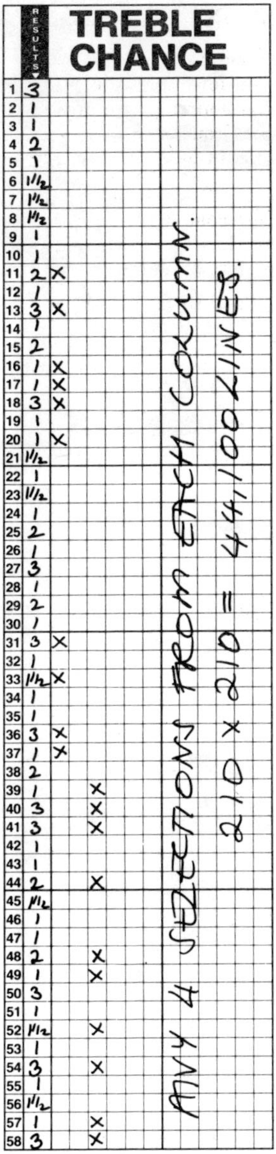

20 SELECTIONS

By far the best method of tackling 20 matches is simply to divide them into two columns with 10 in each.

Any 4 correct forecasts in each column wins 1st dividend.

However the cost of this is way beyond anything the average investor can afford – even on the lowest stake pool.

Nevertheless, any groups or syndicates wishing to make a serious attempt at scoring 24 points might find this full-cover-block perm a worthwhile proposition on the low-stake pool.

Although it takes up 44,100 lines, a full orthodox perm requires no less than 125,970.

For any syndicates opting for this method, mark 10 selections in each of two columns, writing alongside:

Any 4 selections from each column.

210 × 210 = 44,100 lines.

Cost:

Zetters – £29.40

Vernons – £98.00

Littlewoods – £392.00

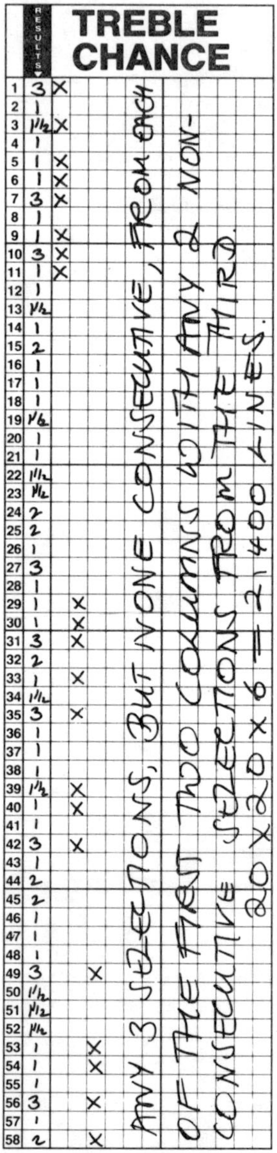

21 SELECTIONS

The success of this perm is dependent on the score-draws not falling in 'clusters'. To cover 21 selections with an ordinary full permutation would require almost a quarter of a million lines (203,490 to be exact).

This method of mine requires just 2,400 with the proviso that within the three blocks of which the perm comprises, none of the score-draws must fall consecutively.

Simply decide on your 21 selections and enter them on the coupon in three columns with 8 in each of the first two, and 5 in the third column – thus making up your 21.

Write alongside your entry:

Any 3 selections, but none consecutive, from each of the first two columns with any 2 non-consecutive selections from the third column.

20 × 20 × 6 = 2,400 lines.

Cost:

Zetters – £1.60

Vernons – £5.34

Littlewoods – £21.34

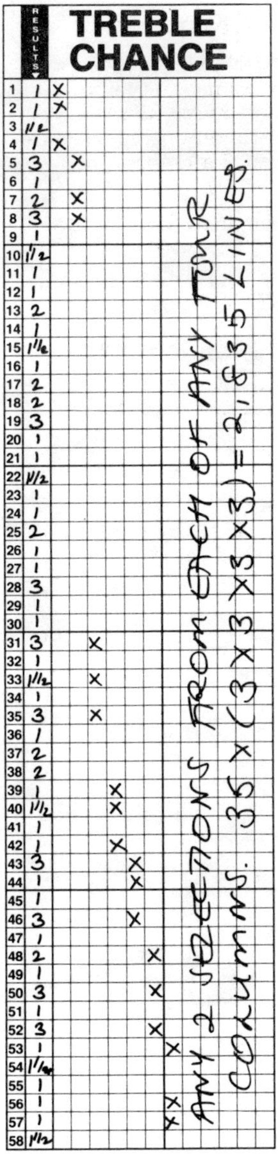

21 SELECTIONS

An interesting yet very economical way of covering 21 matches is to divide them into seven columns with 3 in each.

2 score-draws in each of any four columns will win a 1st dividend.

Just write alongside your seven columns:

Any 2 selections from each of any four columns.

35 × (3 × 3 × 3 × 3) = 2,835 lines.

Cost:

Zetters – £1.89

Vernons – £6.30

Littlewoods – £25.20

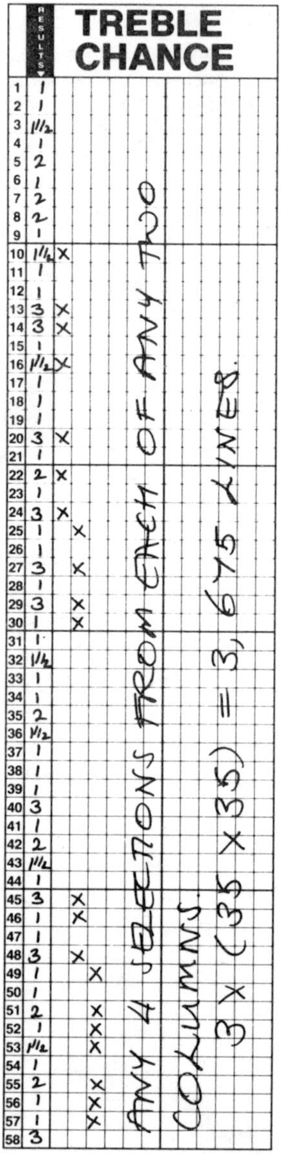

21 SELECTIONS

Another comparatively inexpensive full-cover-block perm which should suit the pockets of many investors on the lowest stake pool, and is 'made to measure' for syndicates on the others, is as follows:

Divide your selections up into three separate columns with 7 in each.

With 4 correct forecasts in each of any two columns you score 24 points.

Write alongside your three columns:

Any 4 selections from each of any two columns.

3 × (35 × 35) = 3,675 lines.

Cost:

Zetters – £2.45

Vernons – £8.17

Littlewoods – £32.67

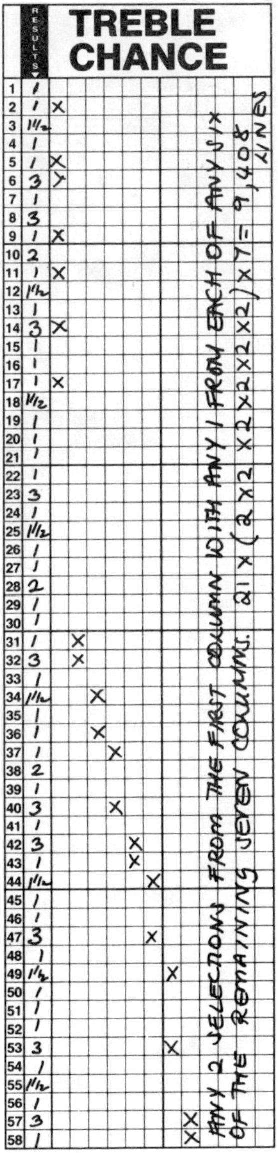

21 SELECTIONS

For a family or perhaps office staff wishing to club together, I can do no better than thoroughly recommend the following method – which should certainly reap dividends throughout the season.

One of the principal virtues incidentally, of this full-cover-block method is that more often than not it will get you off to a flying start, as to 'kick-off' with it entails forecasting only 2 score-draws from 7 selections! Divide your 21 selections into eight columns, with 7 in the first column, and 2 in each of the remaining seven.

Any 2 correct forecasts in the first column with 1 correct in each of any six of the remaining seven columns wins a 1st dividend.

Just write alongside the eight columns:

Any 2 selections from the first column with any 1 from each of any six of the remaining columns.

21 × (2 × 2 × 2 × 2 × 2 × 2) × 7 = 9,408 lines.

Cost:

Zetters – £6.28

Vernons – £20.91

Littlewoods – £83.63

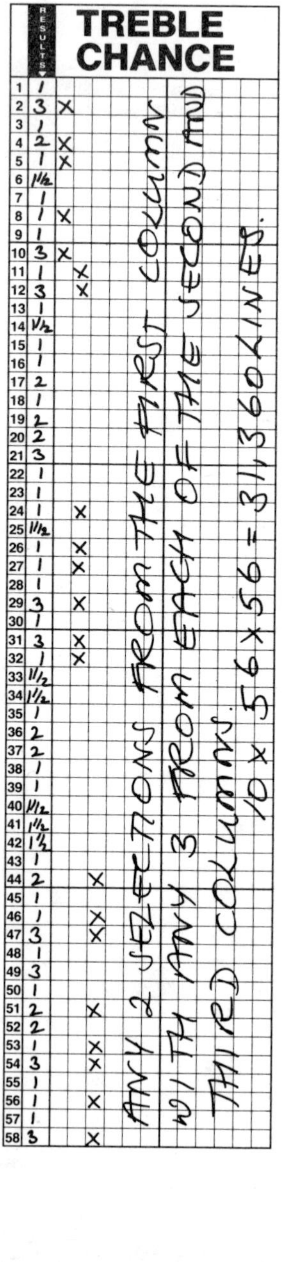

21 SELECTIONS

Another excellent way to deal with 21 matches is a full-cover 3-block perm, which despite taking considerably less than one-sixth the number of lines required of a full orthodox perm, is still out of the question for individuals, even on the lowest stake pool.

However, it is worthy of consideration for large syndicates on both Zetters and Vernons.

Divide your selections into three columns with 5 in the first and 8 each in the second and third.

2 correct forecasts in the first column with 3 in each of the other two will secure a 1st dividend.

Write alongside the three columns:

Any 2 selections from the first column with any 3 from each of the second and third columns.

10 × 56 × 56 = 31,360 lines.

Cost:

Zetters – £20.91

Vernons – £69.69

Littlewoods – £278.76

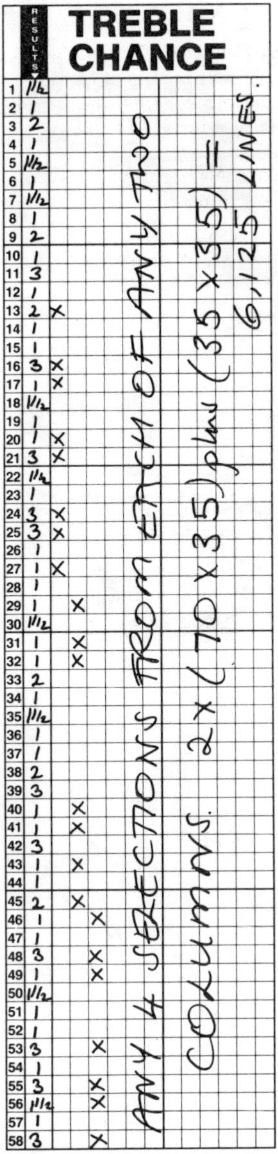

22 SELECTIONS

There are no short cuts to covering in excess of 21 selections inexpensively with full-cover columns or blocks.

Notwithstanding, I cannot advise the use of 'conditional' type plans or perms – the pitfalls of which have already been clearly explained.

There is only one solution, which is to club together with family, friends or colleagues at work and form a small syndicate. After all, sharing 1st dividend achieved by use of a full-cover-block perm must be infinitely preferable to never winning anything at all?

The most economical method I can suggest, and one which will certainly prove fruitful on occasions, is to divide the 22 selections into three columns with 8 in the first and 7 in each of the other two.

Any 4 correct forecasts in each of any two columns wins 1st dividend.

Just write alongside the selections:

Any 4 selections from each of any two columns.

2 × (70 × 35) plus (35 × 35) = 6,125 lines.

Cost:

Zetters – £4.01

Vernons – £13.62

Littlewoods – £54.45

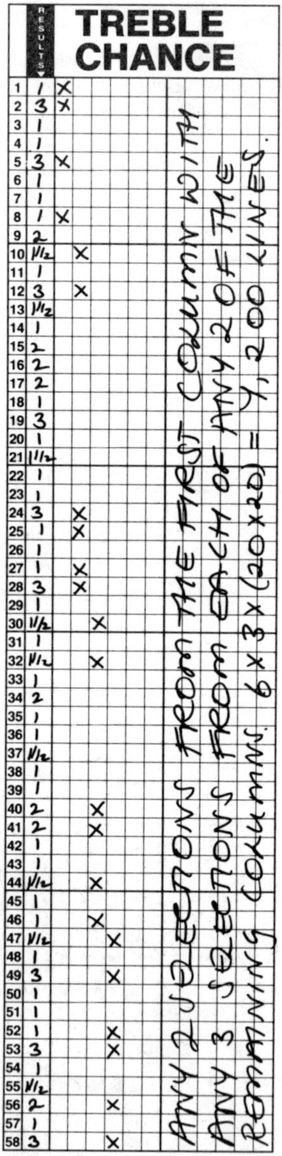

22 SELECTIONS

There is little to choose in actual cost between the 6,125 line perm described on the previous page and the one I am about to suggest.

However, if you are reasonably confident of being able to pinpoint 2 score-draws out of 4 selections, then this one is definitely favourite?

Divide your 22 matches into four columns, with 4 selections in the first and 6 in each of the remaining three.

To score 24 points you must have 2 correct forecasts in the first column with 3 correct in each of any two of the remaining columns.

Write alongside your entry:

Any 2 selections from the first column with any 3 selections from each of any two of the remaining columns.

$6 \times 3 \times (20 \times 20) = 7{,}200$ lines.

Cost:

Zetters – £4.80

Vernons – £16.00

Littlewoods – £64.00

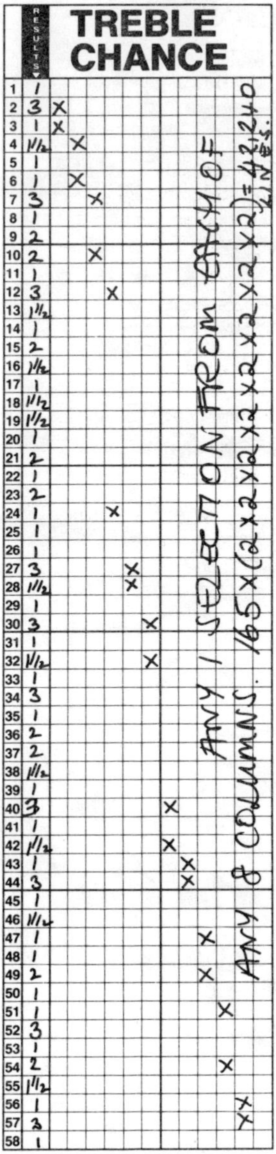

22 SELECTIONS

The following is a viable proposition for syndicates on the lower stake pools, and can scarcely fail to produce dividends sometimes throughout the season.

Divide the 22 selections into eleven columns with 2 in each.

Any one correct in each of any eight columns wins 1st dividend.

Write alongside the columns:

Any 1 selection from each of any 8 columns.

165 × (2 × 2 × 2 × 2 × 2 × 2 × 2 × 2) = 42,240 lines.

Bearing in mind the 319,770 lines required for a full orthodox perm this full-cover each column system must represent value-for-money?

Cost:

Zetters – £28.16

Vernons – £93.87

Littlewoods – £375.47

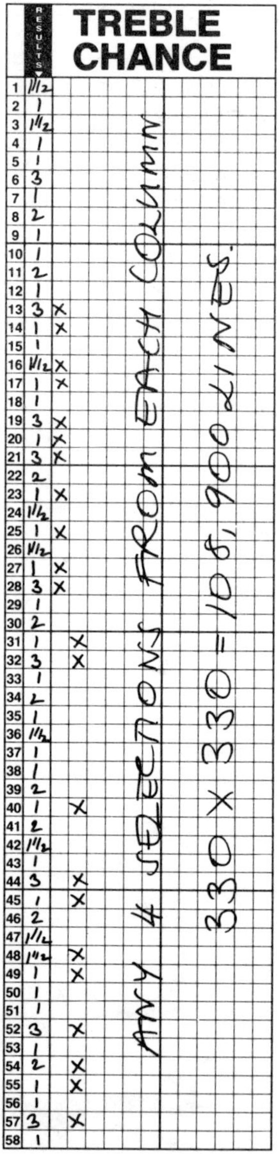

22 SELECTIONS

The ideal method of covering such a large number of selections is by way of a full-cover 2-way block perm, which takes up approximately one third the lines of a full orthodox perm.

This unfortunately is out of the question for individuals due to the enormous cost – but it is a possibility for a large office or works syndicate on the lowest stake pool.

Simply divide your selections into two columns with 11 in each. 4 correct in each column wins 1st dividend.

Write alongside the entry:

Any 4 selections from each column.

$330 \times 330 = 108{,}900$ lines.

Cost:

Zetters – £72.60

Vernons – £242.00

Littlewoods – £968.00

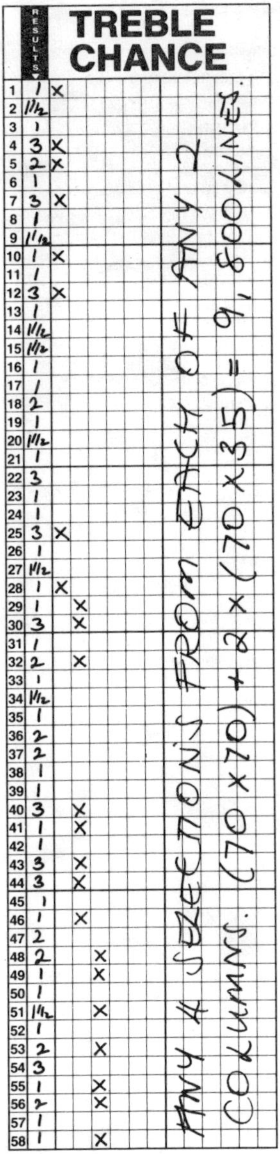

TREBLE CHANCE

No.	Results	Col. 1	Col. 2	Col. 3
1	1	X		
2	1½			
3	1			
4	3	X		
5	2	X		
6	1			
7	3	X		
8	1			
9	1½			
10	1	X		
11	1			
12	3	X		
13	1			
14	1½			
15	1½			
16	1			
17	1			
18	2			
19	1			
20	1½			
21	1			
22	3			
23	1			
24	1			
25	3	X		
26	1			
27	1½			
28	1	X		
29	1		X	
30	3		X	
31	1			
32	2		X	
33	1			
34	1½			
35	1			
36	2			
37	2			
38	1			
39	1			
40	3		X	
41	1		X	
42	1			
43	3		X	
44	3		X	
45	1			
46	1		X	
47	2			
48	2			X
49	1			X
50	1			
51	1½			X
52	1			
53	2			X
54	3			
55	1			X
56	2			X
57	1			
58	1			X

ANY 4 SELECTIONS FROM EACH OF ANY 2 COLUMNS. (70×70) + 2×(70×35) = 9,800 LINES.

23 SELECTIONS

The following method, giving full-cover each column, is ideal on the lower-stake pools for families clubbing together and small syndicates.

It is of course a possibility on the 8/9p line pool but would necessitate a large syndicate.

Divide the selections into three columns with 8 in each of the first two and 7 in the third.

4 correct forecasts in each of any two columns will ensure 24 points.

Write alongside the entry:

Any 4 selections from each of any 2 columns.

(70 × 70) plus 2 × (70 × 35) = 9,800 lines.

Cost:

Zetters – £6.54

Vernons – £21.78

Littlewoods – £87.12

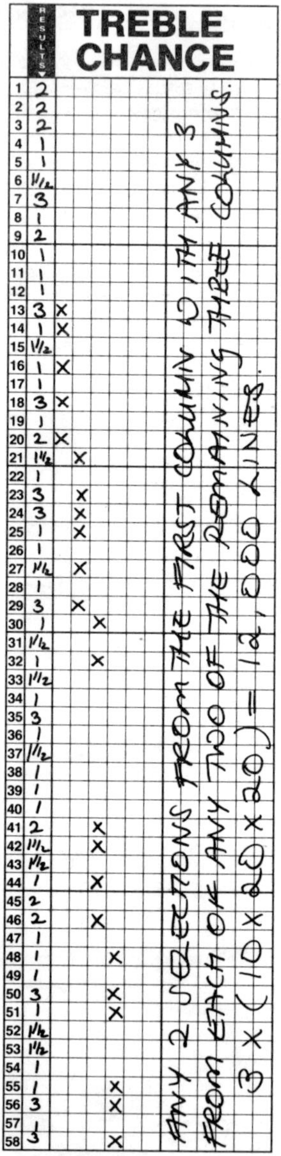

23 SELECTIONS

Slightly more expensive than the system described on the previous page, but again well within range of syndicates etc. on the lower-stake pools.

This time divide the 23 selections into four columns with 5 selections in the first and 6 in each of the other three.

With 2 correct in the first column and 3 correct in each of any two of the other columns you will have 24 points.

Write alongside your entry:

Any 2 selections from the first column with any 3 from each of any two of the remaining three columns.

3 × (10 × 20 × 20) = 12,000 lines.

Cost:

Zetters – £8.00

Vernons – £26.67

Littlewoods – £106.67

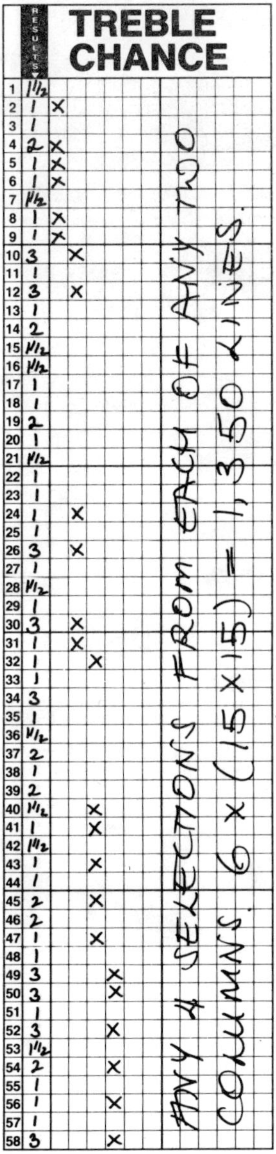

24 SELECTIONS

The following full-cover block method of dealing with 24 matches, if persevered with every week, should make a serious check of your coupon worthwhile several Saturdays throughout the season. Furthermore it should suit everyone's budget on one or other of the pools firm's coupons.

Divide your selections into four columns with 6 in each. Any 4 score-draws in each of any two columns will produce 24 points.

Write alongside your entry:

Any 4 selections from each of any two columns.

6 × (15 × 15) = 1,350 lines.

Cost:

Zetters – 90p

Vernons – £3.00

Littlewoods – £12.00

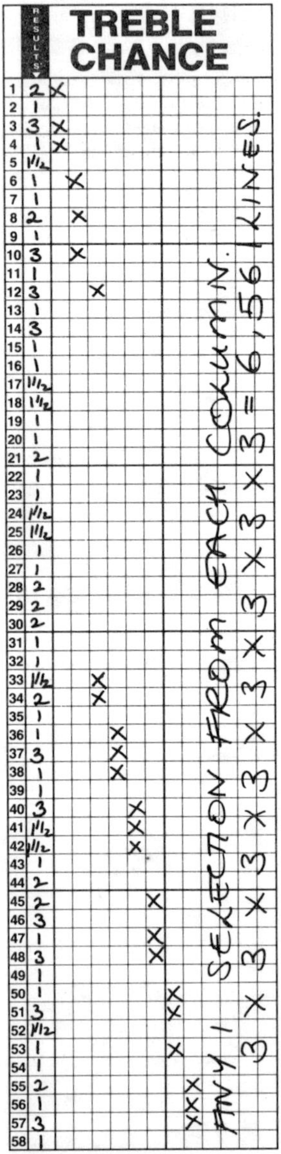

24 SELECTIONS

The following way of dealing with 24 matches is sure to produce dividends, and will undoubtedly appeal to both individual investors on the low-stake pool and syndicates on the higher stakes.

Divide your selections into eight columns with 3 in each. All that is required to win 1st dividend is 1 correct forecast in each column – and with three to pick from each time this particular method presents a very realistic chance of picking up an occasional 1st dividend.

Just write alongside the eight columns:

Any 1 selection from each column.

$3 \times 3 \times 3 \times 3 \times 3 \times 3 \times 3 \times 3 = 6{,}561$ lines.

Cost:

Zetters – £4.38

Vernons – £14.58

Littlewoods – £58.32

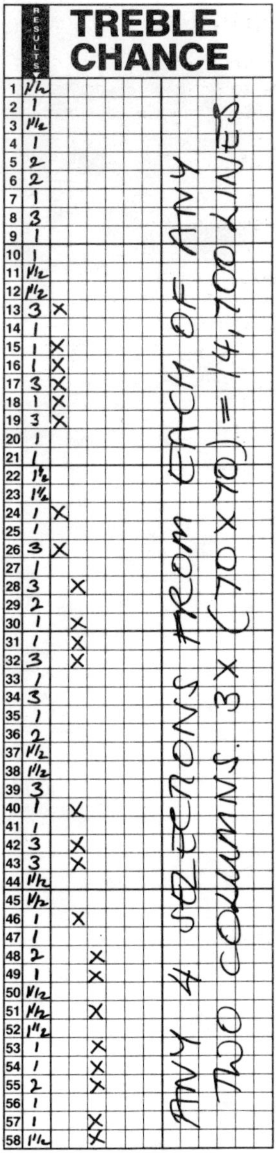

24 SELECTIONS

A full-cover 2-block perm would probably prove too expensive for even the largest syndicates on the lowest stake pool – so the next best way is to divide the selections into three columns with 8 in each.

Any 4 correct in each of any two columns scores 24 points.

Write alongside the three columns:

Any 4 selections from each of any two columns.

3 × (70 × 70) = 14,700 lines.

Cost:

Zetters – £9.80

Vernons – £32.67

Littlewoods – £130.67

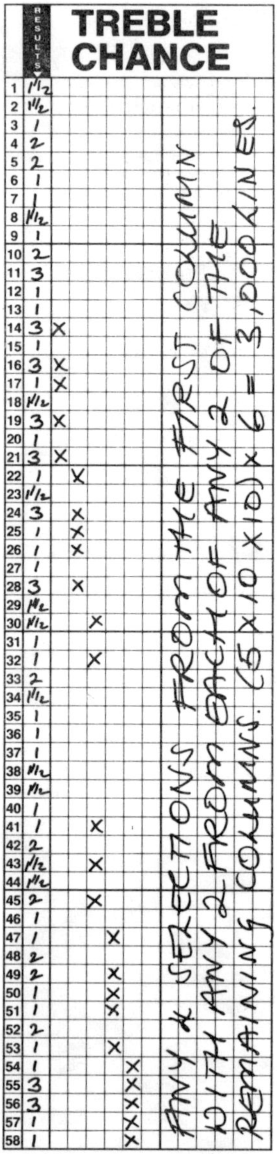

25 SELECTIONS

The following method is inexpensive whilst at the same time gives a realistic chance of picking up dividends.

Divide your selections into five columns with 5 in each.

Any 4 correct forecasts in the first column with any 2 correct from each of any two of the other four columns will net 24 points.

Write alongside your entry:

Any 4 selections from the first column with any 2 from each of any two of remaining columns.

(5 × 10 × 10) × 6 = 3,000 lines.

Cost:

Zetters – £2.00

Vernons – £6.67

Littlewoods – £26.67

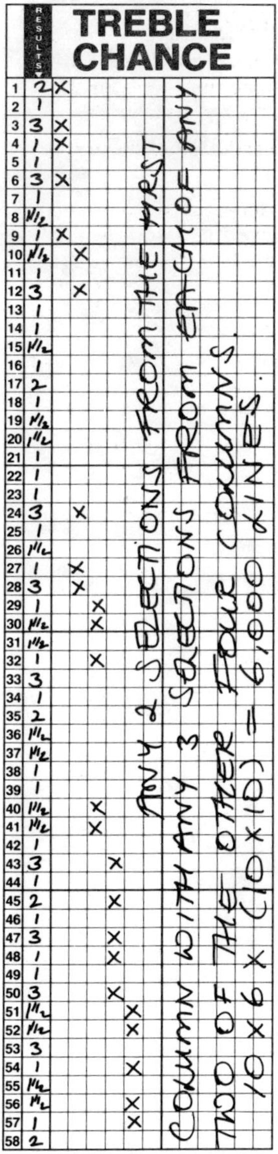

25 SELECTIONS

A very economical way of covering 25 matches and one which at the same time offers a very realistic chance of success is the following:

Divide your selections into 5 columns with 5 selections in each. The first is a 'banker' column in which you must include 2 correct forecasts to score 24 points, together with 3 correct in each of any two of the remaining four columns.

Write alongside your entry:

Any 2 selections from the first column with any 3 selections from each of any two of the other four columns.

10 × 6 × (10 × 10) = 6,000 lines.

Cost:

Zetters – £4.00

Vernons – £13.34

Littlewoods – £53.34

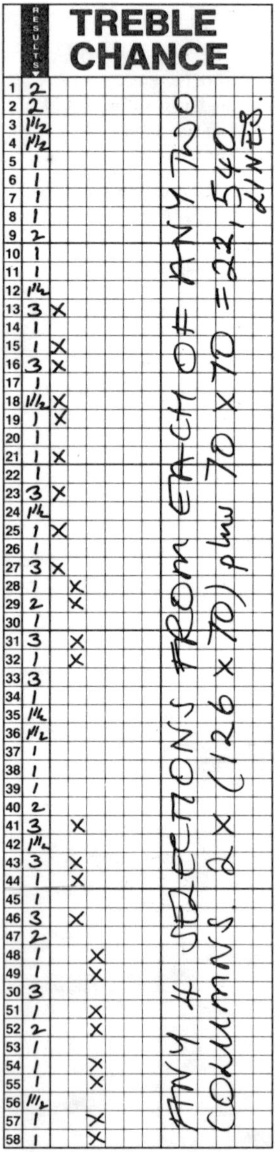

25 SELECTIONS

The following way of dealing with 25 matches may appeal to some large syndicates on the lower-stake pools.

Divide the selections into three columns of 9, 8 and 8.

Any 4 correct forecasts in each of any two columns wins 1st dividend.

Just write alongside the three columns:

Any 4 selections from each of any two columns.

2 × (126 × 70) plus 70 × 70 = 22,540 lines.

Cost:

Zetters – £15.03

Vernons – £50.09

Littlewoods – £200.36

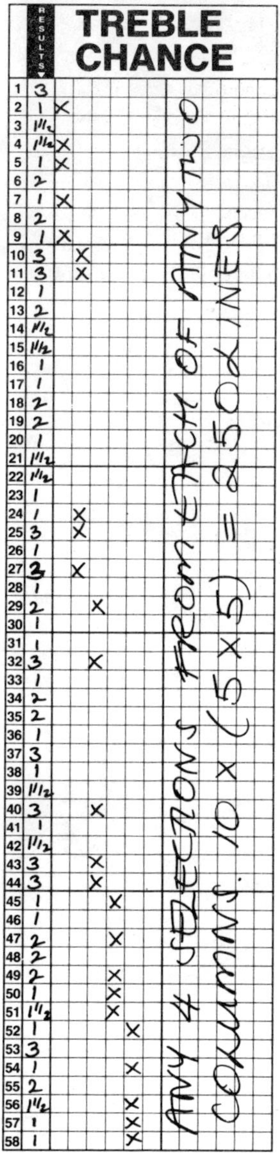

25 SELECTIONS

And now for a little full-cover-block perm which although covering almost half the matches on the coupon, won't stretch the financial resources of even the most hard-up housewife.

Divide the 25 selected matches into five columns with 5 in each.

4 correct forecasts in each of any two columns will win you a 1st dividend.

Granted it's being more than a little optimistic expecting to 'net' 4 score-draws out of 5 selections, but you never know your luck! – and it's all a bit of fun isn't it? Having filled in the 5 columns, write alongside:

Any 4 selections from each of any two columns.

10 × (5 × 5) = 250 lines.

Cost:

Zetters – 17p*

Vernons – 56p

Littlewoods – £2.23

*N.B. As the cost of this perm comes to less than Zetters minimum (25p total pools investment) I suggest having '2 bites of the cherry', and covering 50 matches, i.e. 2 separate entries.

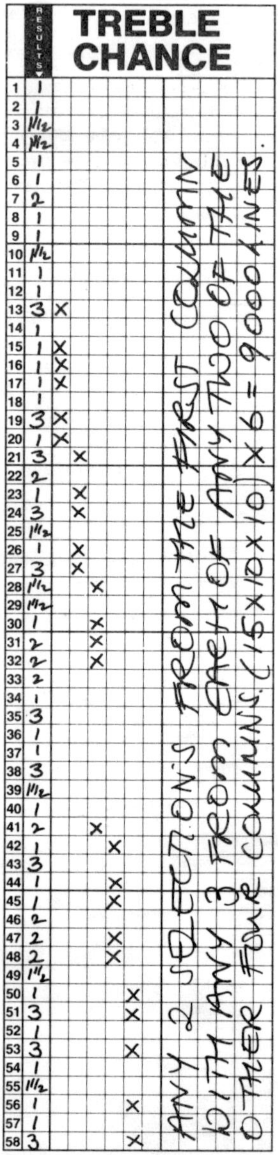

26 SELECTIONS

The most economical method I can suggest – and again it will in many cases necessitate clubbing together with family or friends even on the lower-stake pools, is to divide the matches into five columns with 6 in the first and 5 in each of the other four columns.

Any 2 correct in the first column with 3 correct in each of any two of the other four columns will win 1st dividend.

Write alongside your entry:

Any 2 selections from the first column with any 3 from each of any two of the other four columns.

(15 × 10 × 10) × 6 = 9,000 lines.

Cost:

Zetters – £6.00

Vernons – £20.00

Littlewoods – £80.00

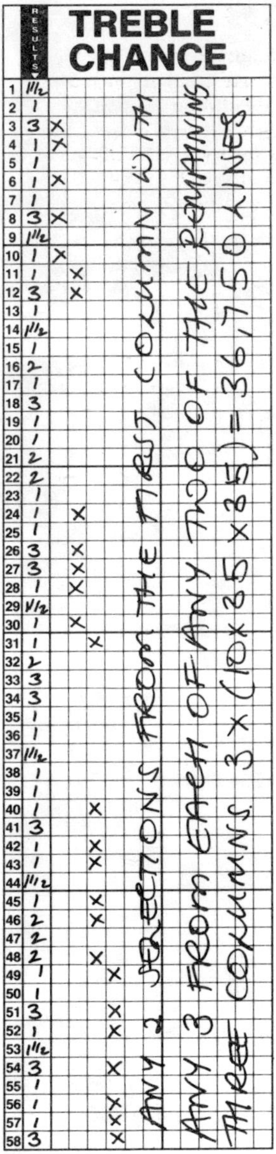

26 SELECTIONS

The following well-balanced method of covering 26 matches is certain to 'bring home the bacon' eventually – providing of course you nominate enough score-draws – which shouldn't be too difficult with so many selections from which to choose.

Again it is expensive but excellent 'value for money' bearing in mind that a full orthodox perm requires over 1½ MILLION lines.

It is beyond the pocket of individual investors but well within the realms of possibility for syndicates on the lower-stake pools.

Divide the selections into four columns with 5 matches in the first and 7 in each of the subsequent three columns.

2 correct forecasts in the first column with 3 correct in each of any two of the remaining columns wins 1st dividend.

Write alongside your entry:

Any 2 selections from the first column with any 3 from each of any two of the remaining three columns.

3 × (10 × 35 × 35) = 36,750 lines.

Cost:

Zetters – £24.50

Vernons – £81.67

Littlewoods – £326.67

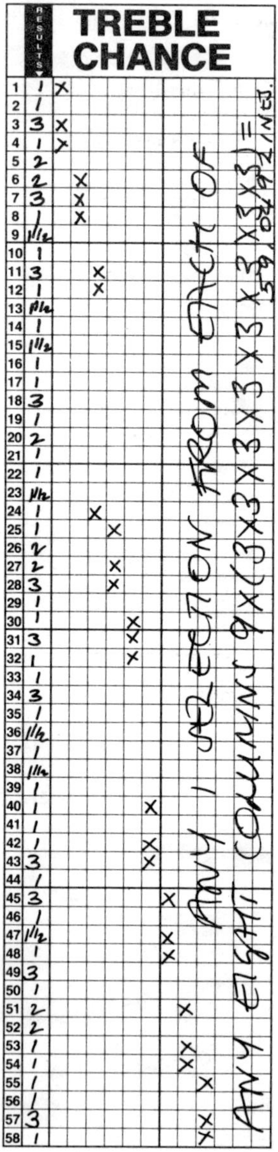

27 SELECTIONS

The best 'value for money' full-cover block method of dealing with practically half the matches on the coupon, but because of the expense is only a viable proposition for large syndicates on the lowest-stake pool is as follows:

Mark off 3 selections in each of nine columns. Any 1 correct forecast in each of any eight of the columns and you have 24 points.

Write alongside the selections:

Any 1 selection from each of any eight columns.

$9 \times (3 \times 3 \times 3 \times 3 \times 3 \times 3 \times 3 \times 3)$
$= 59{,}049$ lines.

N.B. Granted this is a lot of lines – but insignificant compared with the Two and a Quarter MILLION required for an ordinary full perm.

Cost:

Zetters – £39.37

Vernons – £131.22

Littlewoods – £524.88

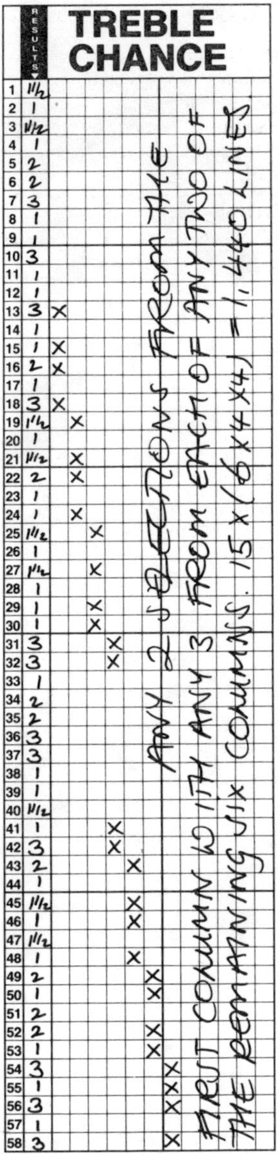

28 SELECTIONS

By using such a large number of matches it is almost inevitable that more often than not you will capture a large proportion of the score-draws on any given Saturday.

On this assumption I think the following economical method, which despite the low cost, still provides for full cover each block, should give rise to plenty of enjoyment and excitement for the investors who like a lot for their money.

Despite having stressed previously that there is no cheap method of covering a large number of matches satisfactorily, I think this particular system could prove the exception.

Divide your 28 selections into seven columns with 4 in each. To win a first dividend you must have 2 correct forecasts in your first column and 3 correct in each of any two of the remaining six columns.

Write alongside your entry:

Any 2 selections from the first column with any 3 from each of any two of the remaining six columns.

15 × (6 × 4 × 4) = 1,440 lines.

Cost:

Zetters – 96p

Vernons – £3.20

Littlewoods – £12.80

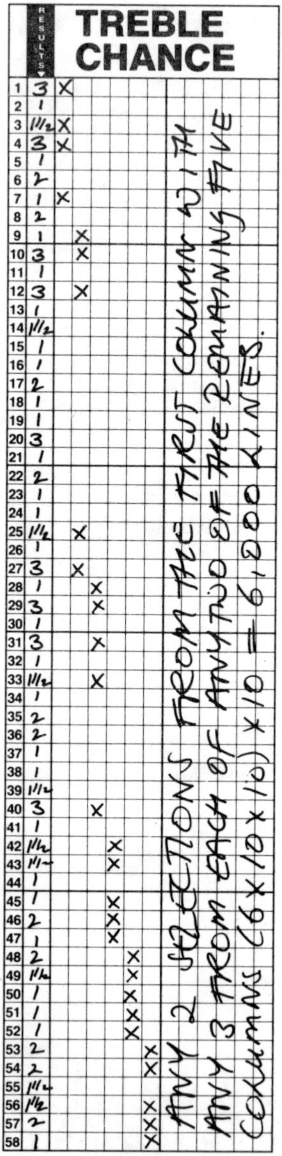

29 SELECTIONS

For a moderate outlay on the lower-stake pools the following method provides plenty of scope for landing that elusive 24 points.

Divide your selections into six columns with 4 in the first and 5 in each of the remaining five columns.

To score 24 points you must have 2 score-draws in the first column with 3 in each of any two of the others.

Write alongside your six columns:

Any 2 selections from the first column with any 3 from each of any two of the remaining five columns.

$(6 \times 10 \times 10) \times 10 = 6{,}000$ lines.

Cost:

Zetters – £4.00

Vernons – £13.34

Littlewoods – £53.34

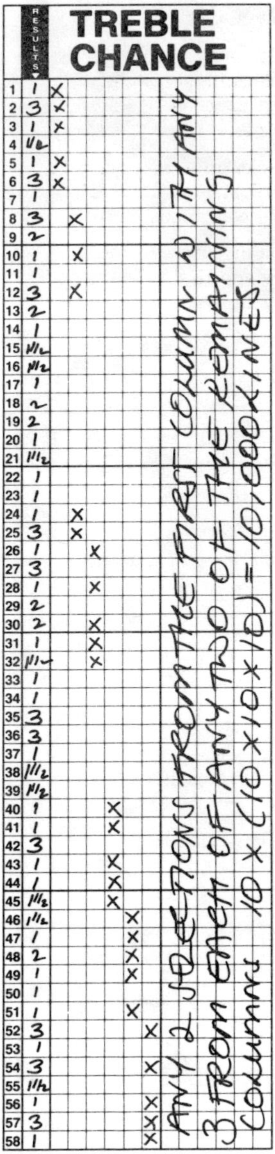

30 SELECTIONS

There quite definitely is no satisfactory way of covering so many matches at a cost which the average investor can afford.

Nevertheless, the following method should be well within the means of families 'clubbing together' on the lowest-stake pool and syndicates on the higher-stake pools.

Furthermore there can be little doubt that on more than one Saturday throughout the season it will give rise to a quickening of the heart-beat at pools-checking time?

Divide the selections into six columns with 5 in each. To score 24 points you must have 2 correct in the first column with 3 correct in each of any two of the remaining five columns.

Write alongside your six columns:

Any 2 selections from the first column with any 3 from each of any two of the remaining columns.

10 × (10 × 10 × 10) = 10,000 lines.

Cost:

Zetters – £6.67

Vernons – £22.23

Littlewoods – £88.89

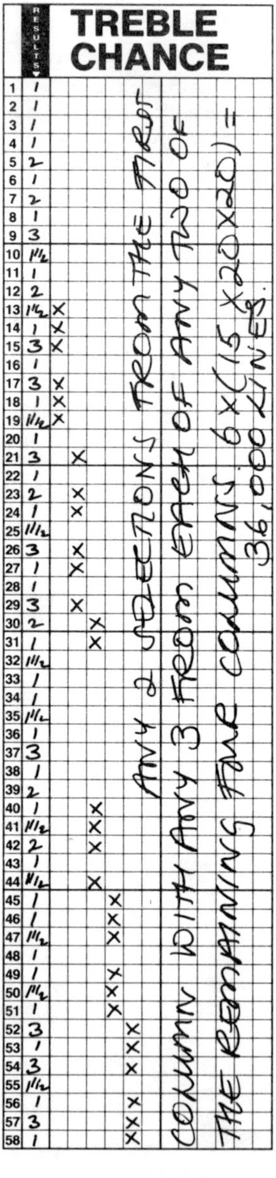

30 SELECTIONS

With over half the coupon covered, by shrewd selecting, investors should frequently 'net' a very high proportion of the total score-draws on the list.

This being the case, the following method should capture plenty of dividends including some 'firsts'.

But again it is only a feasible proposition for syndicates on the lower-stake pools.

Divide the 30 selections into five columns with 6 in each. 2 correct forecasts in the first column (this shouldn't prove too difficult), with 3 correct in each of any two of the other four columns will produce 24 points.

Write alongside the entry:

Any 2 selections from the first column with any 3 from each of any two of the remaining four columns.

6 × (15 × 20 × 20) = 36,000 lines.

Cost:

Zetters – £24.00

Vernons – £80.00

Littlewoods – £320.00

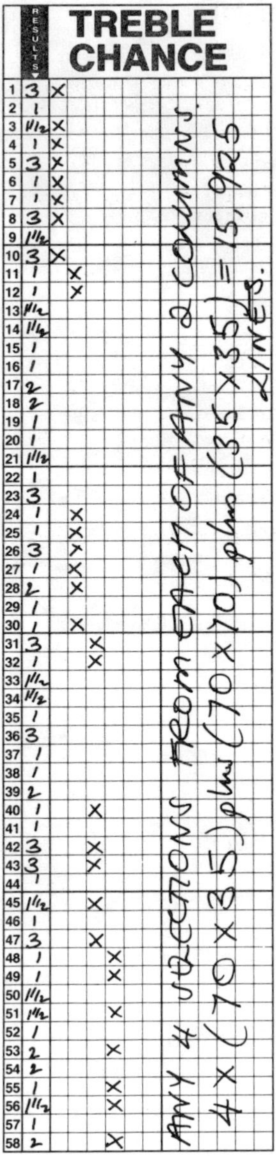

30 SELECTIONS

My third suggestion for coping with 30 matches is again ideally suited to syndicates on the lower-stake pools, and with so many selections covered can hardly fail to produce dividends.

Divide the selections into four columns of 8, 8, 7 and 7.

Any 4 correct in each of any two columns will score 24 points.

Write alongside your entry:

Any 4 selections from each of any two columns.

4 × (70 × 35) plus (70 × 70) plus (35 × 35) = 15,925 lines.

Cost:

Zetters – £10.62

Vernons – £35.39

Littlewoods – £141.56

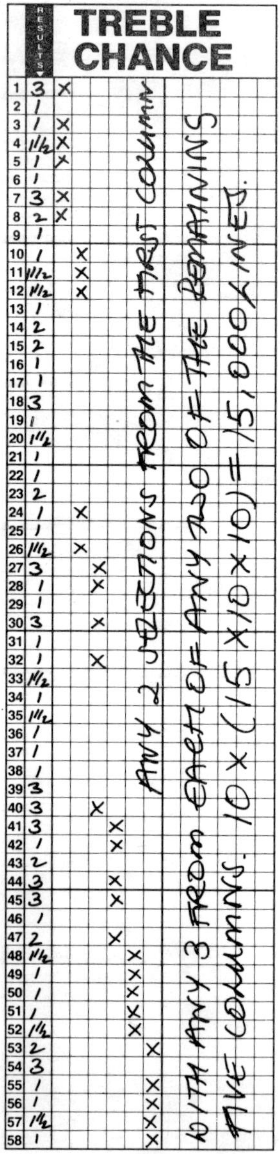

31 SELECTIONS

One method of coping with this odd number of matches is to divide the selections into six columns with 6 in the first and 5 each in the other five.

More often than not, syndicates should get off to a good start with this one, because the first stepping stone to success is to pin-point 2 score-draws in the first column – a target which should be achieved more often than not.

Then in the other five columns you must have 3 correct forecasts in each of any two of them.

Write alongside the six columns:

Any 2 selections from the first column with any 3 from each of any two of the remaining five columns.

10 × (15 × 10 × 10) = 15,000 lines.

Cost:

Zetters – £10.00

Vernons – £33.34

Littlewoods – £133.34

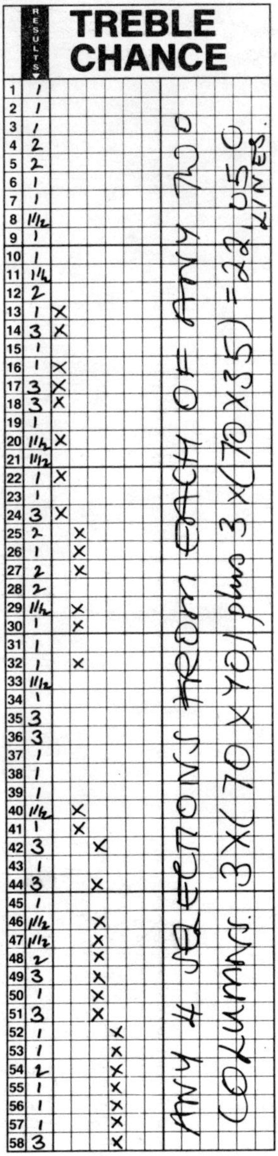

31 SELECTIONS

Another way to deal with this number of matches, but again probably too expensive by far for the individual investor, is to divide the selections into four columns of 8, 8, 8 and 7.

Any 4 correct forecasts in each of any two columns adds up to 24 points.

Write alongside your entry:

Any 4 selections from each of any two columns.

3 × (70 × 70) plus 3 × (70 × 35) = 22,050 lines.

This full-cover-block perm is a feasible proposition for syndicates on the lower-stake pools, but would necessitate the forming of a very large syndicate for entry on Littlewoods.

Cost:

Zetters – £14.70

Vernons – £49.00

Littlewoods – £196.00

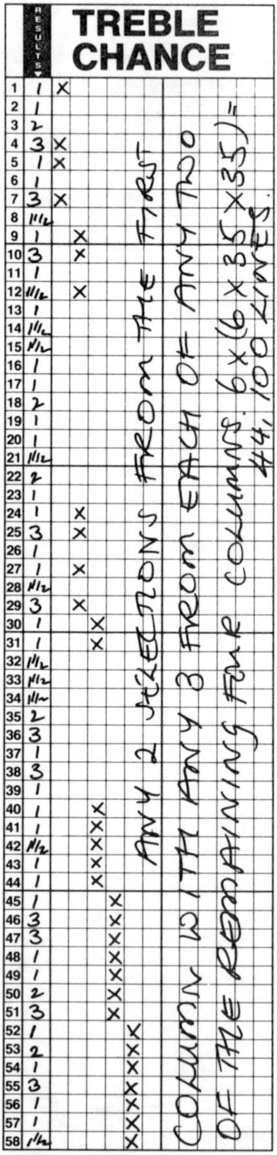

32 SELECTIONS

Syndicates using 32 selections and who heed the advice at the beginning of this book, can be confident of being amongst the dividends several times during a season.

A full-cover orthodox perm for 32 matches requires TEN MILLION FIVE HUNDRED AND EIGHTEEN THOUSAND THREE HUNDRED LINES.

However at a minute fraction of this number of lines this same number of matches can be covered by use of full-cover-block perms, whilst at the same time providing a realistic chance of success.

For my first method, divide the selections into five columns with 4 in the first and 7 in each of the other four columns. 2 score-draws in the first column with 3 in each of any two of the remaining four columns wins 1st dividend.

Write alongside your entry:

Any 2 selections from the first column with any 3 from each of any two of the remaining four columns.

6 × (6 × 35 × 35) = 44,100 lines.

Cost:

Zetters – £29.40

Vernons – £98.00

Littlewoods – £392.00

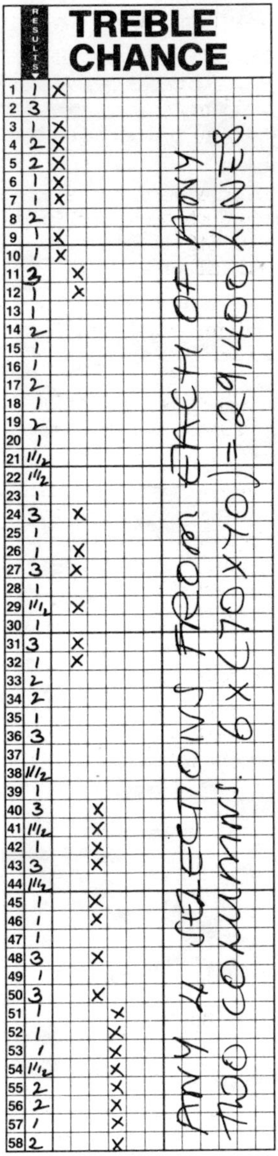

32 SELECTIONS

A less expensive method of covering 32 matches, but nevertheless one with considerable merit, but again one for the large syndicates on the lower-stake pools, is as follows:

Divide the selections into four columns with 8 in each. 4 correct forecasts in each of any two columns gives you 24 points.

Write alongside your selections:

Any 4 selections from each of any two columns.

6 × (70 × 70) = 29,400 lines.

Cost:

Zetters – £19.60

Vernons – £65.34

Littlewoods – £261.34

Whereas I have spent many hours in compiling this book of facts, figures and advice – a combination of which I trust will enable readers to reap some reward from their pools' entries, there is in fact one, and **one only** gilt-edged method of ensuring maximum points on the Treble Chance. This, contrary to the advice preached at the beginning of this book, involves using a full orthodox perm – but I have no qualms about mentioning it because I certainly have no intention of recommending its use. Incidentally however, this particular perm provides the answer to a question which many readers must have posed to themselves sometime or other as they throw away their copy-coupon in disgust following yet another abortive and often frustrating attempt to score that elusive 24 points.

So my final perm, which although of purely academic interest, will undoubtedly provide 'food for thought' and involves the complete list on the coupon.

58 selections

Mark an X alongside every listed match on the coupon and write alongside:

Any 8 selections from 58 = 1,916,797,311 lines (One thousand, nine hundred and sixteen million, seven hundred and ninety seven thousand, three hundred and eleven.)

I'm sure readers wouldn't mind working out the cost of this one for themselves! Incidentally, prior to the increase in coupon matches to 58 the number of lines required would have been only a paltry one thousand, two hundred and seventeen million five hundred and sixty-six thousand three hundred and fifty! By now you will realise why there is rarely an outright winner with 24 points when there are only 8 score-draws on the coupon.

The publishers would be most interested to hear of readers' successes in using the advice and any of the full-cover block perms given in this book.

CHAPTER SIX: DENNIS' PET PERM

The question most often put to me by media interviewers, friends and acquaintances since my first 'pools' book was published, is 'Which method of permutation do you personally use?'. Well, basically I employ a 3-block perm. entailing 21 selections and which has won me hundreds of dividends over the years, including many 'FIRSTS'. Mathematicians, accountants, scientists and other professional bodies dealing with figures are unanimous in asserting that there can be no such thing as a mathematical anomaly. In the context of a football pools permutation I have proved them all wrong!

In fact, a very sceptical accountant friend, after I had expended much time and patience in explaining my 'perm', finally conceded that as far as my system was concerned, I had indeed discovered a mathematical anomaly, something up till then he had thought impossible, and which he agreed must prove of tremendous benefit to pools investors. Although I've been told repeatedly that my 'pet perm' is difficult to understand, it is in truth far less daunting than many of those arithmetical problems which confronted most of us in our schooldays. Nevertheless, should the intricacies of my permutation stretch beyond the mental capability of some readers, then don't worry but just remember the adage ‘there’s not to reason why’ etc. and simply follow my instructions, because many very intelligent people suffer a ‘mental block’ at the very mention of the dreaded words ‘pools permutation’!

There are 31,360 alternatives in which 21 selections may fall using my format comprising two groups of 8 and one of 5 matches. Yet with the exception of a meagre eight eventualities (or patterns), my ‘brain child’ covers the 21 selections in just 10,240 lines! On the face of it, this appears impossible, but ‘seeing is believing’, and this is how it works.

- First of all pick your potential 21 score-draws, and enter them in one column on the coupon.

- Then make a thick dividing line (as illustrated), beneath the 8th selection and again below the 16th selection – thus dividing your 21 selections into three groups comprising eight, eight and five matches respectively.

- The next step is to mark each group ‘A’ against the first, ‘B’ alongside the second and ‘C’ against the final 5 selections.

- The final step applies only to Groups ‘A’ and ‘B’. Simply divide each block of 8 selections into 4 pairs by putting a dividing-line under the 2nd, 4th and 6th selection.

- All that now remains is to write alongside your entry the instructions as shown in the coupon:

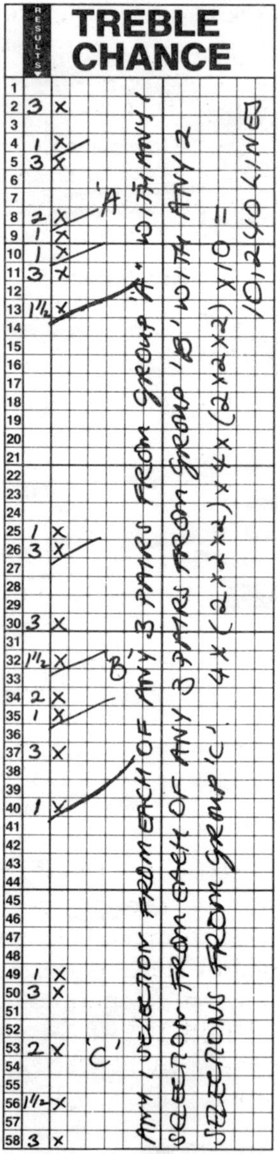

Any 1 selection from each of any three pairs from group 'A' with any 1 selection from each of any 3 pairs from group 'B' with any 2 selections from group 'C'.

4 × (2 × 2 × 2) × 4 × (2 × 2 × 2) × 10 = 10,240 lines.

Cost:

Zetters – £6.83

Vernons – £22.76

Littlewoods – £91.03

This illustrated example includes the hypothetical 'RESULTS' and it may be seen that match numbers 2, 5 and 11 are 'score-draws' in Group 'A' thereby scoring the maximum 9 points. In Group 'B' selection numbered 26, 30 and 37 are '3-pointers' thus gaining the maximum 9 points. And in Group 'C' matches numbered 50 and 58 are both 'score-draws', making in total 9 points in Group 'A', 9 points in Group 'B' and 6 points in Group 'C' giving a grand total of 24 points! Assuming there are three score-draws in each of Groups 'A' and 'B', of your selections then each group must score nine points **unless two of the 'score-draws' fall within the same pair.**

As there are in total only eight PAIRS (4 in each group), then there can be only 8 unlucky eventualities whereby your selections can fail to score maximum points for the groups 'A' and 'B'.

As I pointed out at the beginning of this chapter, to cover these eight 'losing' patterns would cost over three times as much (i.e. 31,360 lines instead of 10,240), which in gambling parlance makes my 'brain-child' an exceedingly good **value for money** wager!

Investors using my 'mathematical anomaly' formula may reverse the order of groups as is illustrated on an actual entry sent in myself. It can be seen from the results alongside that of the 11 score-draws on the coupon my Group 'A' included 2 as required (coupon numbers 15 and 16), in Group 'B' match numbers 41, 45 and 48 each scored 3 points, and in Group 'C' the coupon numbers 49, 51 and 56 each obliged to make up 24 points.

TREBLE CHANCE POOLS CHECK

1	1
2	3*
3	2
4	1½
5	3*
6	1
7	1
8	1
9	1½
10	1½
11	1
12	2
13	1½
14	1½
15	3*
16	3*
17	1½
18	1½
19	1½
20	1½
21	1
22	1½
23	1
24	1½
25	1
26	1½
27	3*
28	1½
29	1
30	1
31	1½
32	1
33	1
34	1
35	1
36	1½
37	2
38	1
39	1
40	1½
41	3*
42	1½
43	1
44	1½
45	3*
46	1
47	1½
48	3*
49	3*
50	1
51	3*
52	1
53	2
54	1
55	1½
56	3*
57	1
58	1

Complete check for all major coupons. Score draw, three points; no score draw, two points; away win or void match, one-and-a-half points; home win, one point.

Caulfield C.	Melbourne	1	
Northcote C.	Morwell	2	
St. Albans	Frankston P.	3	
Doveton	Doncaster	4	
Nunawading	Knox City	5	
S. Oakleigh	Albion R.	6	
Sunbury	Werribee	7	
Bulleen	Hamlyn R.	8	
Keilor	Dandenong C.	9	
Moreland Pk.	Altona City	10	
N. Geelong	Prahran Cty.	11	
Ringwood U.	Sandringham	12	
Royal Richm'd	Essendon C.	13	
Waverley	Eltham	14	
Corio	Coburg	15	X
Geelong	Ferntree	16	X
Pt. Melbourne	Moorabbin	17	X
Prahran	Clifton Hill	18	X
Rosanna	Mooroolbark	19	X
Springvale U.	Bell Park	20	
Yarraville	Yallourn	21	
Boronia	W. Brunswick	22	
Bundoora	Ballaret	23	
E. Brunswick	Clarinda	24	
Hawthorn	Brighton	25	
Karingal	Border	26	
Keysboro	Holland Pk.	27	
Lalor Utd.	Langwarrin	28	
Athena	Gosnells	29	
Bayswater	Osborn Pk.	30	
Kelmscott	Azzurri	31	
Spearwood	Forrestf'ld	32	
Stirling M.	Balga	33	
Bassendean	Kingsway	34	
Cockburn	Kwinana	35	
East Perth	Balcatta	36	
Melville	Fremantle B.	37	
Morley	Queens Pk.	38	
Sorrento	North Perth	39	
Leederville	Booragoon	40	X
Perth City	Mt. Lawley	41	X
Subiaco	Western	42	X
Swan Ath.	Bunbury C.	43	
Swan Crac.	Rockingham	44	X
Wanneroo	Armadale Pk.	45	X
Azzurri	Modbury	46	X
Elizabeth	Camb'ltown	47	X
Polonia	Hellas	48	X
Salisbury	Lion-Grange	49	X
W. Torrens	Para Hills	50	X
Woodville	Croatia	51	X
Cumberland	Pt. Adelaide	52	
Noarlunga U.	Brighton Cty.	53	X
Thebarton	Athelstone	54	X
Westfield	Adelaide	55	X
Windsor	Blackwood	56	X
Croatia	Matric	57	X
Devonport	Launceston U.	58	

'A' 'B' "C"

ANY 2 SELECTIONS FROM GROUP 'A', WITH ANY 1 SELECTION FROM EACH OF ANY 3 PAIRS FROM GROUP 'B', WITH ANY 1 SELECTION FROM EACH OF ANY 3 PAIRS FROM GROUP 'C'. 10 X 4 X (2X2X2) X 4 X (2X2X2) = 10,240 LINES.

Following my 'telephone claim' for 24 points on the Saturday, I received a very useful cheque made up of one 'FIRST' dividend, one second, seventeen 'thirds' and six 'fourths'.

Accountants' Winning Certificate

Certified Dividends for 31ST MAY 1986.

TREBLE CHANCE POOL	£ p	1/15p units	£ p
POSSIBLE POINTS 24.			
24 PTS.	1233.45	1	1233.45
23 PTS.	13.30	1	13.30
22 1/2 PTS.	2.15	17	36.55
22 PTS.	1.50	6	9.00
		10p units	
* 4 SUPER AWAYS.	2.40		
* 4 DRAWS.	8.20		
* PROPORTIONATE DIV. RULE 9B(1)			
		£	1292.30

****
* FOR CRICKET DIVIDENDS *
* SEE ENCLOSED SLIP *
****

All dividends subject to rescrutiny and amendment
8 Match Treble Chance Pool declared to 1/15p units.
All other pools based on units of 10p.

WE HEREBY CERTIFY that the dividends printed above have been duly computed by us in accordance with the current issue of Zetters Football Pools Rules and the provisions of the Betting, Gaming and Lotteries Act 1963.

Kinnaird Littlestone & Co Chartered Accountants

ZETTERS INTERNATIONAL POOLS LTD.

ESTABLISHED IN LONDON IN 1933

THE POOL OF LONDON

40-07-02T

Midland Bank plc

5 Threadneedle Street London EC2R 8BD

4 JUN 1986

Pay DENNIS JONES or Order

The sum of £ 1292—30 £ 1292-30

NO. 4 ACCOUNT

DIRECTOR

For and on behalf of ZETTERS INTERNATIONAL POOLS LTD.

DIRECTOR/SECRETARY

⑈013414⑈ 40⑉07021⑆ 21099604⑈

CHAPTER SEVEN: CHECKING YOUR POOLS

Around 5 o'clock time on Saturday afternoons dreams of Utopia are shattered for millions of punters following their coupon check. Nevertheless, thousands of 'treble chance chasers' find both solace and encouragement on discovering they are 'in the frame' with minor dividends, some of which can be fairly substantial. Sadly many of these investors wait in vain for their winnings cheque to drop on the doormat and assume they must have checked their coupon incorrectly when nothing arrives by the Friday, and they don't bother to claim. This is a mistake which undoubtedly costs many punters thousands of pounds a year, because like all other human beings the 'checkers' employed by pools companies are fallible and every once in a while may make a mistake.

The pools companies **never** deliberately avoid paying out winnings – on the contrary in fact, so if you think you are entitled to winnings and the requisite cheque fails to arrive, then send in your claim as per the instructions on your coupon copy. Incidentally it is advisable to follow up your telephoned claim with a confirmatory letter.

Although personally I have found the pools' checkers pretty competent I have had to send in claims for minor dividends on average twice a year. A typical case in point occurred following Australian matches played on July 20th (1985). There were only 11 score-draws and three no-score draws on the coupon. Claims were required and the dividend forecast was 'Good'. I was just one point short of having to send in a claim, but in view of the 'draw pattern' expected my 2nd dividend with 23 points to be fairly substantial – as was the case.

My winnings failed to arrive by the following Saturday so I telephoned the claims office giving them full details, but on checking their 'winners list' was informed that I was not on it. So either I was claiming in error or their checker was at fault, but I was assured that a further check of my coupon would be made. I followed up my telephone claim with a confirmatory letter and within a couple of days was sent a cheque for £196-05 together with a letter of apology. Had I followed the example of thousands of punters who don't bother to check their coupon but simply wait for the winnings to arrive on the doormat, then I'd have been nearly £200 worse off. So let this particular instance serve as a salutory lesson on the importance of checking your coupon every week and sending in a claim should the need arise.

Vernons Pools

Proprietors: Vernons Organisation Ltd.

Vermail House Ormskirk Road Liverpool L68 1A.
Telephone 051-525 3636 Telex 629142
Telegrams "BETTAPOOL LIVERPOOL"

OUR REF.	YOUR REF.	DATE	51
CJ01/5052/18712	00/000	30TH JULY 1985	

Mr D Jones

Dear Mr Jones

We have pleasure in enclosing your dividend of £196.05p together with 30p expenses incurred in making your claim and regret any inconvenience caused through our error.

Our best wishes are sent for continued success with your investments on our coupon.

Yours faithfully

M. Coleman.

VERNONS POOLS

40-48-03

VERNONS POOLS, LIVERPOOL

PROPRIETORS VERNONS ORGANISATION LIMITED

Vernons Trust Corporation

Vernons Building Mile End Liverpool L5 5AF

Date			Pay to the Order of	£ TEN THOUSANDS	£ THOUSANDS	£ HUNDREDS	£ TENS	£ UNITS	Amount
30	7	85	D JONES	....	......	ONE	NINE	SIX	£196.35

Amount other than pounds as figures

Not Negotiable & Co.

For and on behalf of Vernons Pools

Ref.

Vernon Sangster

⑈038890⑈ 40⑉4803⑆ 00000070⑈

ZETTERS INTERNATIONAL POOLS LIMITED

REGISTERED IN ENGLAND REGISTRATION NO 294864

Telephones:- 01-253 5376/7/8/9 (all lines)

REGISTERED OFFICE AND ALL ENQUIRIES TO

86-88 CLERKENWELL ROAD, LONDON, E.C.1P 1ZS

Date as Postmark

Dear Sir/Madam,

We are in receipt of your recent claim, for which we thank you. Your entry has been re-checked and we have pleasure in enclosing the appropriate winnings, together with a completed Accountants' Certificate

Also enclosed, please find the cost of a first-class stamp to defray the postage you have incurred. May we apologise for both the trouble and inconvenience you have been caused. Please be assured of our careful attention to your future entries. [redacted]

With Compliments,

Yours faithfully,

539 for ZETTERS INTERNATIONAL POOLS, LIMITED

Vernons Pools

Proprietors: Vernons Organisation Ltd.

Vermail House Ormskirk Road Liverpool L68 1AA
Telephone 051-525 3636 Telex 629142
Telegrams "BETTAPOOL LIVERPOOL"

OUR REF.	YOUR REF.	DATE	05
CU01/5053/14258	00/000	13TH SEPTEMBER 1984	

Dear Mr Jones

We have pleasure in enclosing your dividend of £21.90p together with 35p expenses incurred in making your claim and regret any inconvenience caused through our error.

Our best wishes are sent for continued success with your investments on our coupon.

Yours faithfully

VERNONS POOLS

Enc. £22.25p

REGISTERED IN ENGLAND No. 935350 REGISTERED OFFICE 1 BASNETT ST., LIVERPOOL L1 1DZ

CHAPTER EIGHT: BEATING 'SOD'S LAW'

How often does coupon-checking time reveal that practically all the score-draws have fallen in the spaces between your selections? Well, take heart, because providing you can form a syndicate, there is a sure-fire way to exorcise this 'Sod's Law' phenomena once and for all. Although expensive, the antidote I am about to prescribe, will on occasions produce very pleasant 'after-effects' by way of substantial dividends. It necessitates the not-too-difficult task of omitting just **one** match from the coupon – leaving 57 to deal with as per the following instructions.

- Mark off the first 24 selections in chronological order dividing them into 4 columns with 6 in each.

- Then divide each column into 3 pairs with a line under the 2nd and 4th selections.

- Draw a heavy dividing line under the 24th selection.

- Repeat the process with the ensuing 24 matches, and again draw a heavy dividing-line under what will be your 48th selection.

- This leaves 9 Scottish matches (except on the summer coupons) at the bottom of the coupon. Divide these into 3 columns with 3 selections in each.
- Finally mark off the 3 blocks (or sections) 'A', 'B' and 'C' as illustrated.
- All that remains is to write the instructions alongside your entry as per the coupon which follows:

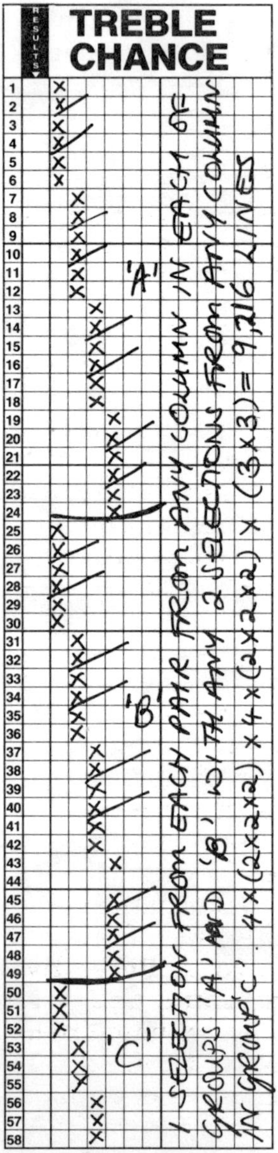

1 selection from each pair from any column in each of groups 'A' and 'B' with any 2 selections from any column in group 'C'.

$4 \times (2 \times 2 \times 2) \times 4 \times (2 \times 2 \times 2) \times (3 \times 3) = 9{,}216$ lines.

Cost:

Zetters – £6.15

Vernons – £20.48

Littlewoods – £81.92

CHAPTER NINE: MAKING THE MOST OF YOUR 'LUCKY NUMBERS'

Birthdates, relatives' ages (providing they're not over 58), house numbers, and telephone numbers are just a few of the **lucky** combinations used week after week and year after year by innumerable investors in the mistaken belief that their numbers must come up sooner or later. Whilst in no way would I deride this method of selection, because every number on the coupon is a potential 'score-draw', the chances of them coming up trumps are, putting it mildly, extremely remote.

Granted that occasionally during the year one hears of an exceptionally lucky punter 'scooping the pool' with just such a 'lucky number' method, but taking these isolated cases in their context, millions of punters have used the same numbers almost since time immemorial and have never won anything worthwhile. Sadly they never will – for the very good reason that the mathematical odds against nominating 8 score-draws from 10 selections are precisely **forty-two million, five hundred and ninety five thousand and four hundred and ninety five.** This is assuming there are just 8 score-draws on the coupon. Obviously the more draws there are, so the chances of winning must increase, but certainly not immeasurably.

Nevertheless, rarely must a week go by when the 'lucky numbers brigade' don't have their appetitite whetted with just a few 'three-pointers' amongst their selections – but how often does a coupon check reveal that despite many of the lucky numbers failing to live up to their 'name tag', their adjacent coupon numbers turn out to be 'score-draws'? So why not put this frustrating phenomena to your advantage? Continue using your favourite selections – which will sometimes produce a few draws, thus providing a springboard towards landing that 'Jackpot'. However, make up the number of selections to 20 by adding an 'X' in each of the squares immediately below your regular numbers.

Should match number 58 be one of your original selections, then mark your 'X' immediately above in 57 – or should two of your original lucky numbers be consecutive, then mark your extra two crosses one above and one below, which will give you four consecutive selections. Having listed your 20 matches on your copy coupon, turn to page 63 and apply your selections on the coupon proper exactly as instructed, marking the first 8 in the first column and so on. Without a vestige of doubt, readers converting to this system will come far closer to landing amongst the dividends (or that elusive Jackpot), than with the method employed hitherto.

CHAPTER TEN: THE LUCK OF THE DRAW

Although I have always enjoyed doing the pools, there is one aspect with which I am less than happy – namely the Pools Promoters Association's method of dealing with postponed matches. Consequently I have written this chapter in order to suggest a better system, one which I believe would have the support of the 16 million pools' investors in the country.

'Every man is the architect of his own fortune' – so said the Roman historian Sallust (86BC-34BC). Unfortunately, the destiny of the millions of pounds of investors' stake monies is controlled utterly and entirely by the pools companies **themselves** whenever they activate their 'pools panel' in order to give the 'results' on postponed matches. Were a referendum to be held amongst the 16 million regular pools' investors on whether they were happy with the present system whereby postponed matches are dealt with by the 'Pools Panel', I am sure the result would be a very emphatic 'NO'. The very mention of 'Pools Panel' is akin to waving a red rag at a bull – and justifiably so, because the system in my view is expensive and unfair. First let me explain to the uninitiated exactly how it operates – and also the approximate cost to the unsuspecting investors of the Pools Panel.

The 'Pools Panel' comprises a team of '6 men good and true' headed by Lord Bath, four ex-top-class professional footballers and a former top-class referee. The presence of Lord Bath is presumably intended to instill confidence amongst pools' investors as to the integrity of the panel and it's methods employed to determine the 'results' of postponed matches. Each member of the 'Panel' is engaged by the Pools Promotors Association at an estimated retainer of £15,000 per annum to travel to the Waldorf Astoria hotel in London (First Class) and remain on 'standby' over the relevant weekends from November until April each year. They arrive at the luxury hotel on the Friday evening with all travelling and subsequent expenses paid and depart on Saturday night or Sunday.

In addition to the Panel's accommodation, the PPA book the 'High Security' suite. The door of this suite is heavily guarded by Securicor on the few occasions when the 'Panel' are ensconced inside whilst deliberating on the results. The idea being that they are entirely isolated from the outside world for the two hours it takes them to decide the destiny of the investors' stake money. Incidentally, in order to preclude any possibility of collusion with any outside sources, the telephones are removed. Taking into account retainers, travelling and the hotel bill, I would estimate the cost of employing the 'Panel' at somewhere in the region of half a million pounds a year – all of which is paid for by the investors.

Although it is inevitable that most weeks the results of matches include the odd 'turn-up', pools investors are entitled to expect a team of footballing experts to forecast **logical** outcomes to the matches with which they deal. Otherwise why should the PPA go to such expense to employ a team of 'experts'? However, the panel's 'results' are often strange, to say the least, as they frequently forecast as 'score-draws' the best-looking 'home' certainties of the day. Not only does this upset the Treble Chance punters but also the millions who also have a flutter on what I call the 'Bread and Butter' pools – i.e. the '10 Homes', '4 Draws' etc.

Even national newspaper pools correspondents, who normally enjoy an amicable relationship with the pools companies and with whom they frequently work in close unison, have started to rebel against the 'Panel' system. Disparaging columns appear regularly to include such comments as that of the *Daily Mail* correspondent who suggested the Pools Companies 'Sort out their own Rule Book'. In fact this same pools correspondent showed admirable restraint when referring to some of their antics as – quote – 'The Pools' Panel's Pranks' – unquote; a piece of alliteration particularly befitting of perhaps one of their most memorable pranks to date and which although executed several seasons ago, will forever remain a candidate for any quiz programme. The question is: 'Which Scottish Premier League team kicked off at 3 pm on their own ground, beating Dundee United 2-0, yet kicking off at the same time, drew away to St. Mirren? Answer: Rangers. Although unbelievable, absolutely true (according to the Pools' Panel.)

For confirmation you have only to delve into the archives and find any Sunday paper dated 17th January 1982, and under the Scottish Premier league results will be seen: RANGERS 2 – DUNDEE UNITED 0, whilst immediately below the results is the Pools Panel list of 'results' one of which is: ST MIRREN v RANGERS – **SCORE DRAW.** How the panel had the effrontery not only to include this match amongst their forecasts, but to make it a score-draw, will forever remain a mystery – because if readers will excuse the grammar, this was the VOIDEST of VOID matches. However, one objective it achieved, and which undoubtedly pleased the pools companies, was a record 'pay-out' pro-rata, for the number of score-draws, for the simple reason that no-one (except perhaps some Standing Entry investors) would have included the void St. Mirren-Rangers match in their selections. In fact the *Daily Express* Pools Correspondent Phil Osborn 'hit the nail on the head' when following a spate of bad weather resulting in subsequent 'panel' forecasts, he said 'quote': 'The Panel's ill-judged conclusions also boosted the dividends to an appropriate level.'

Such has been the discontent of both pools' investors and the media over the current system that in an attempt to 'Pour Oil Over Troubled Waters' the Pools' Promoters Association have finally succumbed to public opinion and decided that their Pools' Panel should adjudicate on *every* postponed match. However, in my opinion this attempt at compromise is totally unsatisfactory, because it applies only to 6 months of the year, whereas the pools' companies issue coupons for 12 months of the year.

At least since the beginning of the 1988/9 season the panel deigned to give a 'result' for every single one of the postponed matches, so punters are no longer subjected to the risk of losing all their money before a ball has even been kicked. However, the safeguard only applies between the months when the panel are on standby (November until April). For the other six months of the year, whenever there are postponements – which could be frequently, the punters' stake money is in real jeopardy. For instance, a very popular full perm entry, particularly on Littlewoods, is the '8 from 10' selections costing 40p. Millions of old-age pensioners and housewives use this particular method because not only is it very inexpensive, but also very easy to fill in. Now supposing there are three or more postponed matches – which is a frequent occurrence, particularly on the Australian pools, and an investor has included at least three of them in an 8 from 10 perm, **then it is impossible to win.** Furthermore, if just one postponed match is included in an '8 from 10' perm, then 80% of the stake money is forfeited, because with only nine selections left, a full perm would only cost 8p. The forfeiture of stake money applies to every punter who unwittingly includes even one postponed match amongst his or her selections. The only remedy for this state of affairs is for a result to be declared for every match listed on the coupon for 12 months of the year.

My dealings with the pools' companies over the last 25 years have given me complete confidence in their integrity, but I must confess that to my mind the 'Panel System' is a grey area which needs urgent reform. After all, why is it that despite knowing full well that even one postponement on the coupon literally sabotages millions of investor's chances, the Pools' Promoters Association steadfastly, and in the face of constant media pressure, refuse to bring their panel into operation for 12 months of the year. However, now they have decided to go through all the paraphernalia of adjudicating on just one postponed match when necessary, they have put themselves in a 'Catch 22' situation! For instance, on the 18th February 1989, there was just one match postponed, and in order to deliberate on this one match, the Panel were presumably locked up in the security suite of the Waldorf Astoria Hotel in London, without any contact whatsoever with the outside world (not even a telephone), whilst they went into a 2-hour huddle to decide the outcome of this one eminent postponed game.

The outcome of this 'pantomime' was a HOME WIN and the match concerned – no less than GOSPORT v ASHFORD! – members of the Beazer League! It would be quite understandable that virtually no-one living outside Hampshire or Kent has ever heard of these teams, but isn't it iniquitous that the investors have to forfeit something in the region of £20,000 in prize money each week in order that a 'result' be determined on a match of such calibre?

There was to be no 'Curtain Call' after the curtain came down on the Panel's final virtuoso performance of the season for matches played on 29th April (1989) – for they were again ONE HUNDRED PER CENT WRONG.

Their lucrative week-end was again marred by just one postponement, namely the Sheffield Wednesday v West Ham match at Hillsborough – a game which in view of their precarious league position, the

'Hammers' could not afford to lose. Nevertheless, the Panel's predictable dividend-boosting verdict was a HOME WIN – actual result played 10 days later – a resounding 2-0 AWAY WIN for West Ham.

Following this 'Grand Finale', the panel were 'put out to grass' for their well-earned six-month rest, yet the following week (6th May) there were FOUR MATCHES OFF – which further endorses my view that to legislate for postponements for only six months of the year is totally illogical and grossly unfair to the 'punters'.

In January 1986 the 'Association of Football Statisticians' published the following information in their monthly magazine. Of 161 panel 'results' forecast during the 1984-5 season, compared against the actual results when the postponed games were eventually played, less than **half** were correctly forecast, and of the considerable number of F.A. Cup matches postponed, **every panel decision was wrong.** To give you two examples. The panel forecast a home win in the case of Newcastle v Leicester and Charlton v Cardiff . . . The actual results were the same in each case – a pair of resounding 4-1 home defeats.

In my view the 'Panel' should be disbanded, and to deal with postponed matches I advocate a method similar to that employed by the Football Association when making the F.A. Cup Draw. To implement my idea, someone – perhaps a well-known personality, but certainly no-one connected with the pools' companies, would attend the BBC or ITV sports studio every Saturday throughout the year. The fee paid to this 'personality' would be infinitesimal compared with the cost of the panel. Equipment required to carry out the operation I am about to describe, would be two black bags (similar to those used by the F.A. when making the cup draw), 58 balls numbered 1-58, each representing a fixture on the football coupon, and finally another 4 balls marked with a 1, 1½, 2 and 3 respectively – each representing a match result – i.e. Home Win, Away Win, No-Score Draw and Score Draw. In the case of any postponements, the appropriate numbered balls representing the coupon number of each postponed game would be placed in one of the black bags, and the 4 balls representing the results placed in the other bag. Then after the classified results had been broadcast, the 'paid personality' would draw a ball out of the bag containing the coupon-numbered postponements, whilst the 'result' would be drawn by the presenter of the Saturday afternoon sports programme (or vice-versa). Not only would this system make for riveting viewing, but it would leave no room for doubting that NOT ONLY HAS JUSTICE BEEN DONE BUT IT HAS BEEN SEEN TO BE DONE.

Readers' Letters

The following is a selection of letters received by the author following publication of the first edition of his pools guide in 1980-1.

'In the past 4 weeks I have won 2 second dividends and scooped 24 points on Vernons – all due to your book.'

(W.A.M., Delapre, Northampton)

'I have read and studied this book with absorbing interest and it makes mathematical sense.'

(R.R., South Harrow, Middlesex)

'Thank you for writing this book – I have been a pools punter for 25 years and it has given me a new aspect altogether.'

(Mrs. D.P., Lelant, Cornwall)

'From start to finish I was delighted with the interesting way Dennis explained about the pools.'

(J.E.T., Sheffield)

'I must thank you for giving me such a lot of pleasure and hope.'

(Mrs. J.T., Formby, Merseyside)

'I am using plans from your book so that I may retire – had a couple of little wins and then I hit the 'Jackpot.'

(J.A., London, NW6)

'Not having done the pools before, I have had my appetite whetted by reading this book.'

(P.J.W., Bridgend, Glamorgan)

‘I do so agree with your theories.’

(Mrs. E.A.B., Brighton)

‘May I thank you very much for writing this book.’

(S.W.K., Retford, Notts.)

‘I have read your book with interest – all the perms are very good and your ideas very practical.’

(E.B., Canterbury)